Mantle Anointing

JUDY A. LITTLEJOHN

Copyright © 2020 Judy A. Littlejohn

All rights reserved. No part of this publication may be reproduced, distributed, or transmitted in any form or by any means, including photocopying, recording, or other electronic or mechanical methods, without the express written consent of the author, except in the case of brief quotations embodied in critical reviews and certain other noncommercial uses permitted by copyright law. Doing so is unlawful according to the 1976 United States Copyright Act. For permission requests, write to the publisher, addressed "Attention: Permissions Coordinator," at the email address below.

ISBN: 978-0-9670791-2-7

Scriptural quotations are taken from the King James Version (KJV), New Living Translation (NLT), New International Version (NIV), Amplified Version (AMP), Contemporary English Version (CEV), and the New King James Version (NKJV). Any references to historical events, real people, or real places are used fictitiously, except where noted otherwise. Names characters, and places are products of the author's imagination.

Book Cover Design by The Brand Chick

Printed by Amazon Kindle Direct Publishing
in the United States of America.

First printing edition 2002
Second printing edition 2021

dr.judybookstudio@gmail.com

www.drjudysbookstudio.com

Welcome Readers!

Thank you for investing in yourself by investing in this work. I believe you are reading the pages of this book because you are in a mantle anointing relationship as either a mentor or mentee, there is a potential for being in such a relationship, or you desire to gain an understanding of how this kind of relationship works. Whatever the reason, you're in the right place.

I encourage you to make notes of what the Holy Spirit is saying to you as you read this book – whether you do so within the pages of this book, in a notebook, or using an electronic device. I have already prayed over this work and for you, believing that the Holy Spirit will illuminate your mind and heart on this journey.

Thank you in advance for telling others about this work and encouraging them to purchase a copy.

Attention to my readers who are writers, authors, and aspirants, no matter where you are in the process, I can help. I offer coaching and individual consulting services through my business, Author Strides, to help you write and publish your story. As a sixth-time author and a one-time Amazon Best Selling author, I take great pride in coaching others in fulfilling their dreams to become an author. *My joy is in helping you!*

Please be sure to visit my website at www.drjudysbookstudio.com, send me an email at dr.judybookstudio@gmail.com, and follow me on social media.
Once you've journeyed through this book, if it has blessed you in any way, kindly leave a professional, positive review on Amazon.com. Thank you in advance.

About The Author

Judy A. Littlejohn is passionate about writing – a skill she started developing in her teenage years when she began formulating concepts and texts. On her literary journey, Dr. Judy started out as an avid expository writer – a skill which has proven both useful and effective as a public speaker when she uses her voice through texts and topics. Dr. Judy's literary skills further evolved into writing a textbook and fictional works. Her writing style and speaking ability are transformative, illuminating both her readers and audience.

Dr. Judy enjoys interior decorating in her spare time, including shopping for housewares and decorative items, walking, word puzzles, and creating and designing documents. She loves animals, geography, and culture to include learning about the cultures of the world. Dr. Judy is a native of Jamaica, West Indies, the youngest of seven, and is a twin. She resides in Massachusetts, in the United States of America.

Visit: www.drjudysbookstudio.com

Table of Contents

Chapter 1
A Mantle Anointing — 7

Chapter 2
Mantle Anointing Relationships ~ Elijah & Elisha — 13

Chapter 3
The Roles of the Mentor and Mentee — 33

Chapter 4
Time Awareness — 39

Chapter 5
Mantle Anointing Relationships ~ Moses & Joshua — 46

Chapter 6
Mantle Anointing Relationships ~ Jesus & His Disciples — 57

Chapter 7
Mantle Anointing Relationships ~ Paul & Timothy — 69

Chapter 8
Male to Female Mantle Anointing Relationships — 74

Chapter 9
Modern-Day Mantle Anointing Relationships — 77

Chapter 10
The Relational Aspect of Reconciliation &
the Fruit of the Spirit — 83

Chapter 11
Covenant Relationships					89

Chapter 12
The Fitting for a Mantle Relationship ~ The Dressmaker		94

Chapter 13
Catching the Mantle ~ from Preparation to Possession		103

Chapter 14
The Mantle Anointing of the Believer				110

Chapter 15
Mantle Anointing and Kingdom Building ~			118
The Power of Two

Chapter 16
Execution of a Mantle Anointing				141

Chapter 17
Wrapping One's Face in a Mantle Anointing			150

Chapter 18
The Anointing and Its Diversity				162

Chapter 19
Obtaining the Mantle Anointing of Jesus Christ		167

Chapter 1: A Mantle Anointing

Preview

The words *"mantle"* and *"anointing"* make a powerful combination. They open up a whole new realm pertaining to team ministry, succession, and continuity in ministry. These words are executionary in nature, implying action.

A mantle anointing is more than a human endowment. It is a divine endowment, which God Himself gives. In mantle anointing relationships, this God-endowed power is used specifically to continue and complete a work that was already begun by someone else. So, the one passing the mantle – the 'thrower' – and the one receiving the mantle – the 'catcher' – not only understands the mission and purpose of the specific tasks but also understands and values the importance of the work already begun and the need for it to continue. In this unique relationship, there is an understanding between both the 'thrower' and 'catcher' about why the relationship exists and what it involves. Additionally, the 'catcher' understands that he or she is being sent with the same kind of anointing and authority as his or her predecessor.

In this unique relationship, the mission becomes amplified and vitally important. One or both parties involved in the relationship can establish the mission based on what the task is. However, for the express purpose of spreading the gospel and winning others to Christ, God has already established the mission based on what He desires and expects of all Christian believers. What is helpful in understanding the mission and how to carry it out is viewing – picturing, looking at it – as a corporate, collective, or joint function and not as an individual function. The church's mission is to spread the message of salvation and bring others to Christ. Our devotion and loyalty as a church should be toward God as we do the work of the Father.

How we accomplish this task depends on what we understand about the work of Jesus Christ and His position in relation to the church, as well as how we are positioned in the body of Christ.

Mantle anointing relationships are Biblical. For example, Elijah and Elisha, Moses and Joshua, Paul and Timothy, and Jesus and His disciples had such a relationship. These relationships are presented in Chapters 2, 5, 6, and 7 of this book.

Definitions

Let's look more closely at the two words that bear the title of this book, *"mantle"* and *"anointing."*

<u>Mantle</u> – A kind of loose garment to be worn over other garments. A cover; to cloke, to cover.

<u>Anoint</u> – To pour oil upon; to smear or rub over with oil… to spread over. To consecrate… to prepare.

<u>Anointing</u> – The act of smearing with oil; a consecrating. *(American Dictionary of the English Language. Noah Webster 1828)*

The definition given for the word *"mantle"* is self-explanatory; however, to put things in perspective, a mantle anointing relationship involves an un-robing from one person to another. It is a relationship of covering. Notice the definition of the word *"mantle": it* says that it is a kind of loose garment to be worn over other garments. In relation to the 'catcher,' this definition embodies the concept of a double portion anointing because the 'catcher' [or successor] does not lose or let go of his or her abilities prior to coming into a mantle anointing relationship. Instead, he or she gains more on top of what he or she already possesses; thus, obtaining a double portion.

The 'catcher's' role may seem paramount to the 'thrower's' role because of the emphasis placed on it earlier, but it is not more important at all. The role or function of the thrower is examined more thoroughly in Chapter 3.

In relation to the anointing, some Christian believers do not fully understand what the word *"anointing"* means [or implies] partly because of a lack of teaching on the subject. Yet, many of them ask God daily for an anointing or greater anointing. For example, we seek the anointing of God in our corporate worship gatherings week after week. What do we expect when we ask for God's anointing? What are we really asking for? It's simple: we are asking for empowerment! We are asking to have an encounter with God that supersedes that which we have already experienced. Sometimes we associate being anointed with the quickening of the body or some type of body movement or gyration. At other times we think being anointed means making a lot of noise and being loud in church gatherings – that the noise constitutes we are having a good time and that God is in the midst, but these things are not necessarily what being anointed means.

The anointing comes upon us strictly to empower us to do a specific work. Acts 1:8 from the Amplified Version of the Bible reads, *"You shall receive power – ability, efficiency and might – when the Holy Spirit has come upon you; and you shall be My witnesses in Jerusalem and all Judea and Samaria and to the ends – the very bounds – of the earth."* Now, here's the 'to do' part: you shall receive power; you shall be My witnesses [tell people about me everywhere].

After reading this verse, there is no doubt about what the specific work is – to tell others about Christ. The anointing does not come upon us to make us feel good, nor does He come upon us to make us run around the church, dance, and speak in other tongues – although, at times, those things will happen.

The anointing comes upon us to drive us to action, to push us! When God releases such an anointing in us, He does so not that it might be contained, but rather that He might be evident in our lives and utilized for the benefit of others. For clarity, let me explain what I mean by the anointing being in us in comparison to our being 'cloaked' with a mantle anointing. The anointing comes upon us like a cloak covers a person's body; however, at the same time, the anointing also resides – is housed – on the inside of every Spirit-filled believer and comes up – flows – out of the inner person. Since being anointed is a divine endowment, we can better understand it as the Holy Spirit's power within us. The Bible says the Holy Spirit has been given to us as God's guarantee that He will give us the inheritance He promised and that He has purchased us to be His own people (Ephesians 1:13-14).

     Some Christians are not allowing the anointing to be released in their lives but, rather, they are keeping Him contained. Once again, holding back may result from lack of teaching and training in this area. The anointing or power of the Holy Spirit is demonstrative, meaning He makes an open show, giving proof of His strength based on the evidence provided through His works. This strength makes it difficult for one to contain the Holy Spirit's power. The anointing of God in our lives is what gives us the strength, boldness, and courage to move forward without being afraid of what the outcome or results of our actions may be. As Christians, our responsibility is to obey God and do what pleases Him. He is Lord over the outcome. Our confidence is in God, not in people, systems, or world beliefs. First John 5:14 says, *"And this is the confidence that we have in him, that, if we ask any thing according to his will, he heareth us:"* (KJV). Although this passage deals with prayer, it relays a very clear message: our confidence assures us that God responds to our requests. If our confidence – assurance – is in God, then who or what can stop us from utilizing the power He has given us to accomplish His work? When the Holy Spirit anoints us for a particular work, He essentially gives us a charge to achieve the mission.

His anointing covers and assures us that we have His divine protection when we obey Him.

Being anointed is an act of consecrating or being consecrated. For example, David was anointed as king over Israel. He went through the formal ceremony with Samuel of having oil put upon him, but the act of being consecrated involved more than this alone (I Samuel 16:12-13). David was set apart for God's calling to a leadership role. God had David consecrated for the office that was His choice for David. Being set apart is what being anointing is all about.

To possess a mantle anointing through the eyes of the 'catcher' – successor – is to wear, utilize, and continue the use of similar ministry abilities as exemplified in the life of the 'thrower' – predecessor – to a greater degree in order to execute and bring to completion a God-ordained mission. Remember these three words: "wear," "utilize," and "continue" because they are important to the message of this book and mantle anointing relationships. In relation to the role of the 'catcher,' to possess this kind of anointing is to become a successor, standing in the place of another.

It's sad to know that some believers sit around waiting for a special assignment or commission when, in fact, they have the greatest anointing ever – the mantle anointing of Jesus Christ. I will discuss this anointing in greater detail in Chapter Fourteen when I address the mantle anointing of the believer. Every believer has been endowed with the mantle anointing of Jesus Christ. Whether or not they know it, that's a different story. We all need to recognize this special endowment.

We have the power, authority, and ability to spread the gospel message according to the unique gift or ministry abilities God has bestowed on us.

Surveying our surroundings should prompt us each to ask God, "How do You want to use me?" As we make ourselves available to God, He will equip us with what we need to accomplish the task.

      Having examined the two words *"mantle"* and *"anointing,"* we now have a better understanding and will be able to grasp the relationship conveyed throughout this book – God has empowered [anointed] us to continue a work already begun. Thus, we must remember what a mantle anointing involves.

Chapter 2: Mantle Anointing Relationships ~ Elijah & Elisha

Elijah and Elisha Meet

"And the Lord said unto him [Elijah], 'Go return on thy way to the wilderness of Damascus: and when thou comest, anoint Hazael to be king over Syria:

And Jehu the son of Nimshi shalt thou anoint to be king over Israel: and Elisha the son of Shaphat of Abelmeholah shalt thou anoint to be prophet in thy room.

And it shall come to pass, that him that escapeth the sword of Hazael shall Jehu slay: and him that escapeth from the sword of Jehu shall Elisha slay.

Yet I have left me seven thousand in Israel, all the knees which have not bowed unto Baal, and every mouth which hath not kissed him.'

So, he departed thence, and found Elisha the son of Shaphat, who was plowing with twelve yoke of oxen before him, and he with the twelfth: and Elijah passed by him, and cast his mantle upon him.

And he [Elisha] left the oxen, and ran after Elijah, and said, 'Let me, I pray thee, kiss my father and mother, and then I will follow thee.' And he [Elijah] said unto him, 'Go back again: for what have I done to thee?'

And he returned back from him, and took a yoke of oxen, and slew them, and boiled their flesh with the instruments of the oxen, and gave unto the people, and they did eat. Then he arose, and went after Elijah, and ministered unto him." (I Kings 19:15-21, KJV).

Names

There are those who are inseparable. They work well together and appear to be a perfect fit. Elijah and Elisha were such a pair. There must have been glitches in their relationship along the way, but the Bible doesn't paint that picture for us. The understanding we gain from their relationship is: God puts people together in mantle anointing relationships. Such relationships go beyond those merely for our personal enjoyment and satisfaction – they go beyond just friendships. In other words, mantle anointing relationships don't exist just so people can feel good about having close friends. These relationships exist because God has a purpose and a mission that must be accomplished. His intention is to complete His mission through those He has joined together in this kind of relationship or partnership.

Knowing God's intention, let us examine the relationship between Elijah and Elisha. The name *"Elijah"* means 'The Lord is God.' Elijah was a prophet. As such, he represented God to the people. The prophets of the Old Testament were living epistles, which the apostle Paul speaks of in II Corinthians 3:2-3. They conveyed the word of God, which was delivered from God's mouth to their ears. Old Testament prophets continually received divine messages from God. These messages came by way of a warning, a judgment issued, a future blessing, or call to repentance. Staying in close fellowship with God, in a place where God could speak to them, was important for prophets.

The first mention of Elijah is found in I Kings 17:1, which says that he was a Tishbite from Gilead. Elijah served in the Northern Kingdom [Jerusalem] during the reign of Ahab.

Elijah was a man of prayer. He had strong interests in education, and he continued the schools of the prophets founded by Samuel. He also instructed Elisha in administration.

Elijah and Elisha were acquainted before Elisha received the call to be Elijah's successor. In fact, Elijah schooled Elisha. The "sons of the prophets" regarded Elijah with respect and affection (II Kings 2:7, 15, 16-18).

Elijah's unhesitant devotion to the Lord made him a bold spokesman for what was right. God gives us boldness, and prophets must be bold about speaking what God says (Ephesians 3:12, 6:19; Hebrews 4:16, II Corinthians 3:12). Elijah was a man of great character, making him an ideal candidate for God to use, not that God doesn't use flawed individuals. Character is what God develops in us when we surrender to Him (Romans 5:3-5).

Concerning Elisha, the name *"Elisha"* means "God is salvation." Elisha was the son of a man named Shaphat of Abelmeholah. His name appears in I Kings 19:16, as the one Elijah was instructed to anoint as his successor. Elisha, too, served primarily in the Northern Kingdom, from the latter reign of Ahab into the rule of Joash. Like Elijah, Elisha had a prophetic anointing – he was God's mouthpiece. Elisha eventually proceeded with the same type of ministry anointing that Elijah had. For example, serving the schools of the prophets, helping the needy, performing miracles, and acting as a spokesman for God. All the things Elisha did, proved him to be the successor of Elijah. God knew exactly what He was doing. They were truly a match made in Heaven.

Through Elijah's name, we understand that the Lord is God. Conversely, Elisha's name reflects a fuller, deeper revelation of God – God is salvation. In the meaning of their names, we see the mysterious workings of God. Elijah and Elisha had twin spirits. God endowed them with the same ministry anointing, which Elisha furthered – having a double portion – upon Elijah's departure from earth.

Here are two crucial lessons from the meeting of Elijah and Elisha.

1. Instruction

Before God took Elijah away, He instructed him to anoint Elisha as his successor. Does God give this kind of instruction today? Perhaps the better question is: Do we obey Him when He does?

It is a sad commentary when leaders move on in life to do other things, leaving behind no one as their successor because they did not take the time nor see the importance of training others. We cannot grasp the significance of training and preparing others until we first understand and embrace that God calls more than one person to a gift, office, or ministry. (See I Corinthians 12:4-11; Romans 12:6-8 and Ephesians 4:11-13 for a list of gifts).

2. Special Selection

Elijah threw his mantle on Elisha because Elisha was God's choice of a successor. But let's look at this more closely. Who better to be Elijah's successor than the one he had trained in his school of prophets? Through training, Elijah put his spirit in Elisha. But it doesn't stop there because one can have someone's spirit to do or continue a work but do nothing with it. God, in his infinite wisdom, knew Elisha was trained well and that he wanted a double portion of Elijah's anointing.

In my devotional book, *Reset with God*, I talk about the difference between needing someone and wanting someone. Wanting someone is better. Training allows the trainer to deposit his or her spirit into the trainee. That's what Elijah did with Elisha. A prospective successor cannot continue the work of a predecessor – and expand it – without having that person's heart. A vision becomes divided – [di]vision – when an individual goes against the one with the vision.

The prefix 'di' means apart, asunder. Elisha's heart was knitted with Elijah's. He was ready for a double portion of Elijah's anointing. Here's how we know. First, Elisha asked for it. Second, he did what Elijah told him to do – he kept his eyes on Elijah so that when Elijah was taken away in the whirlwind, Elisha saw it. Elisha's heart was single – he was solely devoted to the work of Elijah.

Not everyone will have the prerogative of being in a human relationship like that of Elijah and Elisha and others whom I will discuss in later chapters. However, those who know the Lord have the mantle anointing of Jesus Christ in the person of the Holy Spirit. I only hope they know it.

Some individuals serve as a bridge between the prospective predecessor and the prospective successor, giving access to an individual to whom the prospective successor may not otherwise have access.

That individual enables the one who has been 'fitted' for a mantle anointing relationship to more easily identify with the right person, stepping into a relationship with a bit more ease.

A mantle anointing is unique because it is not something that arbitrarily happens. It is divinely orchestrated and established by God. For this purpose, God matches or pairs up and empowers individuals to share in a ministry work. Furthermore, they may be contemporaries in a task. Such individuals have kindred spirits, meaning they are drawn to each other and have a heart – desire and passion – for the same things (I Samuel 18:1). A knitting of souls occurs between those with kindred spirits. As a result, it is challenging to part those with whom a special closeness, bond, and friendship have been established.

After God orchestrates the initial pairing up and those involved recognize and respond to such a pairing, they then have the responsibility to cultivate the relationship, so they can move forward effectively to accomplish the specific task God has assigned them to.

To be endowed with a mantle anointing is not a human appointment; it is a God-connection. In other words, it is not merely a coming together by human agents; it is pre-established by God. Those who fit the profile simply need to yield to what God is doing and follow His lead. When God pairs people together in this kind of special relationship, others take notice bearing witness to the special connection.

3. Obedience
Elijah received instruction from God to anoint Elisha in his place, and he obeyed God. As stated earlier, God makes the connection between those He destines to be in mantle anointing relationships. Furthermore, He does so because this kind of relationship is too important for us to have our human hands in it. It is God's business.

Elijah and Elisha obeyed God. They encountered challenges along the way, but because their responsibilities as God's prophets were paramount in their lives, they did the will of God regardless of the obstacles they faced.

The lesson here is that the task must be more important than the person or people involved – more important than the challenges faced. Accomplishing God's work on earth requires a special recognition of the role we play in His grand plan. Doing God's work helps to give us a proper perspective, placing emphasis on the One who called us to the task, not on our personal preferences.

A balance between being people-oriented and task-oriented is critical within the local church. People-orientation involves caring for souls, bringing the gospel message, and servicing others. Task-orientation consists of identifying the needs – short-term and long-term – prayerfully selecting and assembling those who are best suited for the task, creating and implementing a plan with achievable goals, executing the work efficiently, effectively, in God's time – depending on what the specific task is – and implementing checks and balances throughout the entire process.

A good question to ask is: Who are we accommodating as we begin a task? Is it God or others? Honestly, the answer is both, but God should always be at the forefront. The first step to accommodating God in a task is by seeking Him for it. Yes, that's right. We don't know what's on God's mind, and we don't always know what He wants us to do, so seeking Him is not optional – whether that be through studying the Bible, prayer, worship, quieting ourselves in His presence, extending ourselves to others, or all of them. The second step is yielding to God, especially when He reveals and/or clarifies what the task is. Many tasks have come to a halt because priorities are out of order. The main thing is to focus on God and what He has commissioned us to do.

Obedience is essential in our vertical relationship with God and in our horizontal relationships with others, including mantle anointing relationships. The truth is obedience brings victory and success in our lives (I Chronicles 14:16-17).

4. Work
When Elijah found Elisha, Elisha was working. This tells us that God uses those who are prepared and those who make themselves available. God uses those who are willing to work and give of their time, talents, and treasure.

Consider the Parable of the Talents found in Matthew 25:14-30 and Luke 19:11-27. Furthermore, the book of Proverbs 10:26 says, *"Lazy people are a pain to their employer: they are like smoke in the eyes or vinegar that sets the teeth on edge"* (NLT).

God calls upon those whom He can trust to carry out a task or assignment to completion, not that they are perfect or unflawed but, instead, their heart is right towards Him. A willingness to work, commitment to the task – let's be clear: God uses people to assign tasks – and a level of excellence by which the task is performed, matters.

The message of The Parable of the Talents is this - we must be good stewards. We must use what God has given to us without fear, to bring glory to Him. Otherwise, others will receive a reward that could have been ours. God is patient, but He will not hold up His Kingdom work waiting on us.

5. Pursuit

The first time Elijah threw his mantle on Elisha, Elisha wanted to follow him, but it wasn't yet time. This account is found in 1 Kings 19:19. Here, the gesture signified that Elisha – at the appointed time – would continue the work of God as begun through Elijah. It's a gesture that may seem strange to those who don't understand it, but Elisha understood the significance of it.

When Elijah threw his mantle on Elisha, Elisha ran after him. He didn't walk. Running here speaks of pursuit, a key factor in mantle anointing relationships on the part of the catcher. In recognizing his need to advance in his calling, Elisha pursued Elijah. He understood what needed to happen to make the transition; thus, he responded immediately.

Elisha didn't allow anyone or anything to come between him and Elijah (II Kings 2:2-6).

Although God called Elisha to the prophetic office, He used Elijah as an agent in grooming Elisha through their special relationship. As I said earlier, God uses individuals to assign tasks and to help establish a work in the lives of others.

The second time Elisha handled Elijah's cloak was after they had been separated by a chariot of fire and horses when Elijah was taken away. Elijah had already told Elisha that if he saw him being taken away, a double portion of his anointing would be his. This account is found in II Kings 2:9-13.

Elijah knew that Elisha would succeed him. God had already told him so (I Kings 19:16). I am merely speculating as to whether God decided to replace Elijah because he was ridden by fear of Jezebel and her threat against him for defeating the prophets of Baal (I Kings 18 and 19) or whether God put a plan in place to protect Elijah and spare him from being killed by appointing his successor and taking him away in a whirlwind, or both. Whichever the case, the laugh was on Jezebel.

Individuals who are in a mantle anointing relationship should recognize it early on and value the relationship to the end. Faithfulness and loyalty are preservatives of such a relationship.

The loyalty that mentees exhibit toward mentors relay a powerful, unspoken message. A true mentee is not influenced against his or her mentor by the negative opinion of others concerning the mentor and their relationship.

The reason is because there's a commitment that's based on what the mentee knows about the mentor's life, character, experiences, relationship with the Father, and more, far beyond what others *think* they know of the mentor. The adage, "blood is thicker than water," is familiar to many, placing value on family relationships and their strength and loyalty. Similarly, spiritual mantle anointing relationships reveal this truth. The story of David and Jonathan depicts this loyalty, although their relationship was a covenant one. When God pairs people together for His purpose in a mantle anointing relationship, tearing it apart is difficult. There is a divine draw, a divine purpose.

I personally know of a modern-day mantle anointing relationship between two people that cemented many years ago. For the purposes of this writing, I will not reveal their names, but I had the pleasure and privilege of being around them many times as they would come to my city to serve God's people through the teaching and preaching of His word. One was an evangelist and the other was her armorbearer. In this case, they did not know each other on a personal level prior to connecting. In sharing with me how they became connected, the one who became the armorbearer was in a church service where the evangelist was ministering the Word of God. It was not her first time hearing her speak as she frequented services when the evangelist was brought into town, and I could see why. She knew there was to be an extraordinary relationship. Like Elisha, the armorbearer-to-be pursued the evangelist.

One evening following a church service, she managed to get face-time with the evangelist, and she said these words, *"Hi, Naomi. I'm your Ruth."* That's it. From that very day, she became the evangelist's armorbearer. She left her own life as she knew it, relocated to the city where the evangelist lived and traveled with her, serving her faithfully and loyally everywhere she went. At that time, I had not seen anything like that.

The armorbearer helped her in every way – driving her to speaking engagements across the country, ironing the woman of God's clothing once they arrived where they would lodge. I know this because I hosted them in my home once. As soon as they arrived, the armorbearer took their luggage to the spare bedroom, unpacked the evangelist's clothes for the evening service, ironed them, and then went straight to bed without having a bite to eat or anything to drink. I was amazed at such loyalty, service, and discipline. I learned that was their practice whenever they traveled, which was all the time. It was important for the armorbearer to get adequate rest since she was doing all the driving, leg work, and serving the evangelist. After she napped, she had something to eat and drink.

Another thing I observed between the two was that the armorbearer didn't speak much – not when the evangelist was on assignment. She served her quietly. If I initiated a conversation, she would talk with me, but even then, the conversation was light and brief. It was important to the evangelist that her armorbearer didn't engage in idle talk as her role was also to cover the evangelist in prayer while on assignment. Additionally, she was a spiritual watchwoman for the evangelist. When I tell you that was a divine appointment and a mantle anointing relationship, believe me. I got to witness it firsthand. The armorbearer's name became synonymous with the evangelist's name. As they travelled, she was given the same level of respect as the evangelist. People knew she was the gateway to the evangelist.

What I loved about the armorbearer was that she was in the relationship wholeheartedly with no ill motive. She wasn't trying to make a name for herself or get into the evangelist's personal business. No, the relationship was pure – as pure as they come. Even if her motive was wrong, it wouldn't have worked – not with that particular evangelist.

Today – in the 21st Century in the year Two Thousand and Twenty – the armorbearer is still with the evangelist, only their titles and roles have changed, long before now. The evangelist married her high school sweetheart and became a pastor. It was at that time that she discontinued road ministry, as we called it. She was and still is greatly missed by those of us who know her ministry. In due time, she was elevated to the office of a bishop who is well respected and in high demand. As for the armorbearer, for her faithfulness and loyalty to the evangelist, God blessed her with a husband and they made a beautiful family together. She is currently the finance director in the bishop's church, amongst other roles of honor and trustworthiness. The anointing on her life is equal to that of the anointing on the bishop's life – only in different roles – because she faithfully served the Lord by serving the bishop for many years. There was a passing of the mantle from the mentor to the mentee. I visited them at the bishop's church and witnessed with my own eyes and ears God's favor, blessings, and grace upon their lives.

Loyalty doesn't betray, lie or deceive; it protects, defends, and *in some cases* where appropriate, 'covers' an individual's faults and flaws. On the part of the mentee, loyalty goes beyond majority opinions or actions against the mentor without knowing and understanding the facts. The same is true vice versa except that the mentor isn't obligated to being loyal in the same way as the mentee.

The role loyalty plays on the part of the mentee when the mentor is proven at fault in a situation *can* be challenging to define as circumstances differ. Does the mentee still have the responsibility of remaining loyal to that individual? He or she may, but that depends on the situation and the 'fault.' At the very least, the instruction given in Galatians 6:1-2 should be put into effect.

Dear brothers and sisters, if another believer is overcome by some sin, you who are godly should gently and humbly help that person back onto the right path. And be careful not to fall into the same temptation yourself. Share each other's burdens, and in this way obey the law of Christ. (Galatians 6:1-2, NLT).

Keeping all things in proper perspective, we should take into consideration what the situation is, the person's position who has caused the problem, how bad the situation is, and how many people have been adversely affected by it. We can restore each other, but some form of discipline may also be necessary. Nonetheless, even in such a case, the mentee should maintain his or her integrity and seek God on whether loyalty to the mentor is a wise choice, or space is needed for repentance and correction. Being loyal to someone should never be at your detriment. In cases where the mentor is suffering for the cause of Christ, the role of the mentee is to remain loyal to the mentor through good and bad times, supporting the mentor with even *more* prayer. Such demonstrated loyalty, however, does not advocate supporting those who *willfully* and *consistently* choose to sin, disobey God, or refuse to receive and apply wise and godly counsel.

In such a case, the mentees' responsibility is to protect their own integrity and disassociate himself or herself from the mentor who chooses to continue in sin because then, the mentor has clearly chosen another path other than a godly one. In fact, a mentor can no longer serve *respectfully* in this role – or any role – with a life that reflects sin and disobedience. Willful, repetitive acts of sin cannot be ignored. The same is true vice versa.

Mantle anointing relationships are more profound than superficial, surface friendships. A deeper bond and connection are present that causes both people to stick together, allowing nothing to separate them.

6. Fathering

Elisha viewed Elijah as his spiritual father. Elisha looked to him for spiritual guidance and nurturing (II Kings 2:12). Spiritual fathering is not just a man's role; it is a woman's role. Spiritual fathering has to do with nurturing and is a non-gender role. Additionally, it has to do with mentoring, grooming and leading others by example. In the natural realm, fathering has to do with one who has learned valuable lessons from life's experiences and can share those lessons with others. Fathers care for and love those whom they father. They are unselfish with their resources, give wise advice, and are not afraid to rebuke the children. Isaiah 38:19 says that the role of the father is to make known the truth to the children. Fathers do not keep their children in darkness!

For many people, the image of ideal fathers is of those who are strong and provide provision and protection for their family, yet, at the same time, are tenderhearted and compassionate towards the needs of their family. Fathers have the responsibility of watching for the safety of their family as well as providing for the overall needs of the household.

7. Preparation and Timing

Elisha said something significant to Elijah. He said, *"...First let me go kiss my father and mother good-bye, and then I will go with you!"* (I Kings 19:20, KJV).

Although Elisha was anointed to be Elijah's successor, he knew that God meant this special act of consecration as his time to follow and serve Elijah, not to lead. In other words, Elisha recognized and respected God's order. Just because God anoints us for something does not mean we are ready to take the lead in that area or office. Preparation is involved. When Elisha went after Elijah, he did so to serve him. Furthermore, this kind of serving was also to prepare and teach Elisha lessons.

Preparing and learning are the stages most people are anxious to get beyond because patience and hard work are required (I Kings 19:21).

Some want to lead but not follow. Great leaders are first good followers. The benefit of Elisha following Elijah was that he would have the opportunity to learn first-hand by observing the things Elijah did on a daily basis. Undoubtedly, Elijah had excelled in areas that Elisha had not yet mastered. The mentor typically is more experienced and more refined than the mentee, but that depends on how seasoned the mentee is at his or her current level of ministry or work.

While Elijah's ministry continued, Elisha served him. Elisha did not focus on himself or what he wanted to become. He focused on Elijah and supported what God was doing in and through him. There's always the temptation of wanting to jump in the driver's seat when finding out you will become a successor. Acting hastily is not God's way concerning mantle anointing relationships such as what Elijah and Elisha had. God's way is that the mentee waits patiently and prayerfully as he or she prepares and develops himself or herself for positions of leadership. God will initiate the timing of the passing of the mantle.

Elisha knew he would get his chance at taking the lead, and I personally believe that was not his focus. He sincerely wanted to be fathered by Elijah and to serve him. Being a servant also enabled Elisha to see more closely what Elijah did and how he did it. It allowed Elisha to see from the inside out rather than from the outside in. Such closeness also gave Elisha the opportunity to ask questions, just as the relationship between Jesus and His disciples gave room for questions.

The important message in these observations is that Elisha had to serve and minister to Elijah as part of his training in order to know what it would take to fill Elijah's shoes.

Lessons from the Continuation of the Story

8. Transition from Servant to Leader
The next time we see Elisha's name is in II Kings 2:1, which marks the beginning of the account of Elijah's ascension to heaven.

When the Lord was about to take Elijah up to heaven in a whirlwind, Elijah and Elisha were traveling from Gilgal (NLT).

Elijah tried, on three different occasions, to leave Elisha behind, but Elisha would not allow a separation to occur. The last three places Elijah and Elisha traveled were significant to the transition that would occur in both of their lives. Elisha was aware that his time was near to become Elijah's successor. He knew how important it was to stay at Elijah's side in order to successfully complete the final stage.

Second Kings 2:2, 4 and 6 from the New Living Translation reads as follows:

And Elijah said to Elisha, "Stay here, for the Lord has told me to go to Bethel." But Elisha replied, "As surely as the Lord lives and you yourself live, I will never leave you!" **So, they went down together to Bethel**.

Then Elijah said to the Elisha, "Stay here, for the Lord has told me to go to Jericho." But Elisha replied again, "As surely as the Lord lives and you yourself live, I will never leave you." **So, they went on together to Jericho**.

*Then Elijah said to Elisha, "Stay here, for the Lord has told me to go to the Jordan River." But again, Elisha replied, "As surely as the Lord lives and you yourself live, **I will never leave you." So, they went on together**.*

The story places significance on the three places God sent Elijah.

First Stop: Bethel

The Hebrew name *"Bethel"* literally means *"House of God."* Bethel also served as a worship center in Biblical days. At Bethel, the prophets of that area approached Elisha, confirming what he already knew – God was going to take Elijah away.
When we are in the right place at the right time, with a worshipful attitude toward God, He reveals things to us and confirms what He has already made known to us. Worship of the Lord then becomes a powerful tool in our lives. Worship is the avenue to receiving divine revelation and mysteries from God. The purpose of God sending Elijah to Bethel was really for Elisha's benefit. God wanted to confirm to Elisha those things that would take place in the life of Elijah. In this way, Elisha could get himself ready for the transition from servant to leader.

We can miss out on opportunities to hear from God when we are not willing to travel – symbolically – to Bethel, which signifies that we are not in the 'right place' to hear from God. A spiritual implication exists in this viewpoint – the words "right place" doesn't necessarily mean physical location as they do one's frame of mind, spirit, maturity level, and attitude. Just as the Bible contains figurative, literal, and symbolic language, so does this book.

Second Stop: Jericho

Like Bethel, Elijah's brief visit to Jericho was also for Elisha's benefit. The prophets of Jericho approached Elisha to confirm that Elijah would be taken away soon. Such confirmation marked the second time Elisha received this message, which meant God had established it, and Elijah's departure was impending. Likewise, God sends confirmations to us regarding a task, role, or future blessing that He has in store for us.

The most notable aspect about Jericho is its main attraction – a spring – which existed in ancient Jericho and still exists in modern-day Jericho, watering the greenery of the land.

The spiritual significance of *this* spring in connection to Elisha is that God sent him through this region so the water – life of God – could flow through him as he prepared to become Elijah's successor. Something else was at work here – at this point in time, at the Jericho stop, Elisha had to be willing to become transparent as water. In other words, Elisha had to examine himself at Jericho, making sure that his main goal was to accomplish more for God and not to outdo Elijah. Desiring more of God and a greater anointing is good, but we must also make sure that our motive is not for selfish reasons. Jericho was an important stopping point for Elisha to obtain the mantle anointing of Elijah. At important 'stopping points' in our lives, God shows us ourselves prior to advancing us to other tasks. Such introspection is salient as it helps us to know what lies on the inside of us and what we need to work on.

Third Stop: Jordan River

At the Jordan River, Elijah did something he had not done at the previous two places – he folded his cloak [mantle] and struck the water with it. The river divided, allowing him and Elisha to go across on dry ground (II Kings 2:8). The item used at the Jordan River crossing was Elijah's mantle, which was a symbol of his prophetic authority.
Elisha would mimic the use of the mantle later on. God takes us to special places and connects us with exceptional people to show us what He is getting ready to do through us. Exposure of this magnitude is principal if we're going to walk in authority when the time comes.

The Jordan River (and not another river) has significance in this story. The name *"Jordan"* means *"go down"* because the river descends and loses altitude rapidly. Thus, it signifies that it was time for Elijah to go down or decrease so that Elisha could come up or increase, fully functioning in Elijah's place. The time had come for Elisha to experience an increase by receiving the mantle of Elijah!

The parting of the Jordan signified the beginning of Elisha's ministry and the ending of Elijah's. Elijah, recognizing his end was near, asked Elisha, *"What can I do for you before I am taken away?"* Elijah could not have asked this question at Bethel or Jericho; it was not the right time. Having already examined his motives at Jericho, Elisha requested to become Elijah's rightful successor. The request was granted unto him by God. Herein lies three lessons: 1) Promotion comes from God; 2) The anointing for the task or to fill the role comes from God, not man; 3) We should not be afraid to ask God and then others for what we need if it's something that will help us step into our rightful place.

In summary, God sent Elijah to Bethel – the house of God – to worship Him and for Elisha to receive confirmation from God through the other prophets. Then he sent Elijah on to Jericho as the final stage of preparation for Elisha prior to his receiving Elijah's mantle. Finally, God sent Elijah to the Jordan River, where the initial 'changing of the guards' would be carried out.

Think of it this way:

Bethel = The House of God = Worship = Revelation and Confirmation from God

Jericho = God Establishes His Word = The Spring = The Life of God = Transparency = Self-examination

Jordan River = Exercise Authority = Ascent of the 'Thrower' of the Mantle = Succession of the 'Catcher' of the Mantle

In traveling to Bethel, Jericho, and the Jordan River, Elisha was determined not to let Elijah out of his sight. He was a true servant to the very end. Most people would be eager to move on and not stay to the end of a particular assignment or task. After Elijah proved Elisha's faithfulness, devotion, and commitment to the call, he said, *"...Tell me, what can I do for you before I am taken from you?"* (II Kings 2:9, KJV). Elisha valued his relationship with Elijah. Not even Elijah's departure could truly separate them. He knew Elijah would be taken away from him and that his final moments with Elijah would be the most crucial part of the relationship and the succession transition. Above keeping his eyes on Elijah when he was taken away, I believe that as a result of Elisha's sensitivity to the process and loyalty to Elisha, he received what he asked for – a double portion anointing.

Chapter 3: The Roles of the Mentor and Mentee

Mentors

We need to know our role when God has called us into mantle anointing relationships. The responsibilities of the mentor are to know the mission and purpose, be able to effectively communicate it with passion to the mentee, and function as a spiritual parent, effectively leading the mentee to his or her assigned role as successor. The mentor must be passionate about the mission; otherwise, he or she will not effectively train and equip the mentee with what is needed to continue it. The mentee's responsibilities include lining up with the mission so that he or she can carry it out effectively and efficiently. In Chapter Fourteen, we'll look at Jesus Christ as our perfect role model for relationships.

Our posture in prayer should be one of asking God for sensitivity and awareness of this kind of relationship throughout the body of Christ. God may not endow you with the mantle of another, but He may be calling you to cast your mantle on another. Just as this kind of relationship existed between Elijah and Elisha, there are men and women alike in Christendom who are equipped to foster such relationships with those upon whom God has chosen for them to 'cast their mantle' or receive a mantle.

Mentors must believe in God's purpose for them – the call – and know how to communicate knowledge of that purpose to others. Furthermore, they must be secure in calling others unto themselves. Salient to the role of mentors is being secure. Understanding the call to replicate and embracing the notion of being replaceable are foundational concepts to the role of mentors.

Mentors must be mature enough to see into the lives of mentees in terms of their abilities – developed and undeveloped, revealed and hidden – and recognize both the good and not so good in others. Moreover, availability is a crucial factor in the role of mentors. They must be available and willing to make room for and invite mentees to shadow them – train them – as mentees come into their lives. By default, this means being open. Such openness may mean not having as much privacy as one might be accustomed to or like – on either part.

The mentor is responsible for issuing 'the charge' to the mentee as David did to Solomon before he died (I Kings 2:1-9). The value of having a spiritual mentor is indispensable. For this reason, if the mentee does not follow the God-given advice of his or her mentor, then failure, destruction, or a curse can occur (II Chronicles 24:17-20). In no way does this mean mentors have the final say or overrule God. No! It simply means God has given authority to mentors, and when He connects a mentor with a mentee, as long as the mentor remains in God and hears from Him, then that person can speak into the mentee's life with the assurance that God has given him or her the authority to speak. Accordingly, true spiritual mentors give wise counsel, and mentees would do well to receive and heed their counsel (Proverbs 1:8-9, 13:20).

The mentor-mentee relationship also resembles that of companionship, which has great value (Ecclesiastes 4:9-12). Companionship provides opportunities for sharing, learning, and getting to know one another beyond what appears on the surface. Let's look at some examples.

Paul and Timothy

Paul and Timothy are a good Biblical example of a mentoring relationship. Timothy was a young minister and pastor in need of instruction and guidance. Paul was more experienced and mature than Timothy, spiritually and naturally, and was well suited to instruct Timothy in both aspects of his life. Paul took Timothy under his wings like a father would a son. Mentoring is parental in nature.

As a mentor, Paul counseled and encouraged Timothy in the work of the Lord as they were important for Timothy's spiritual growth. In fact, in Paul's pastoral letters such as I and II Timothy and Titus, he gave Timothy the guidance he needed. Paul mentored Timothy in areas such as recognizing and responding to false teachers, having faith in Christ, and making worship public with an emphasis on the importance of prayer. Additionally, Paul helped Timothy to understand church leadership. He invested in Timothy's overall growth with a desire to see Timothy succeed personally, spiritually, and pastorally.

Mentoring requires the mentor to take the mentee as his or her own. Paul referred to Timothy as *"my own son in the faith"* (I Timothy 1:2). The relationship between mentor and mentee should be close. Paul mentored Timothy in areas specific to his calling and role. Likewise, he also mentored him pertaining to conduct and various disciplines. These valuable lessons included knowing how to guard his motives, standing firm in his faith, living above reproach, and ministering faithfully.

To his death, Paul mentored Timothy passing him the torch of leadership and encouraging him in the faith. Additionally, Paul left his protégé – Timothy – a powerful charge – *"preach the word!"* Mentors must charge or challenge mentees.

Accountability

Accountability is necessary between mentors and mentees because neither party is independent of the other but, instead, united together for a specific purpose. Each person must know what the other is doing and thinking, which means that this kind of relationship has little space for independence and privacy.

There are would-be successors who have not yet been ushered into a particular work or role because some mentors are afraid to impart what they know into the lives of others. In part, I believe this results from abuse of information on the part of mentees and unregulated authority and power. Nonetheless, mentors have the responsibility of empowering, equipping, and releasing – or imparting – into the lives of their mentees. Doing so is critical, so the work of God will not be hampered when the 'thrower' transfers the responsibility to the 'catcher.' In short, the mentor's responsibility to the mentee is to give counsel, guide, tutor, or coach, all the while exhibiting trust toward the mentee and being a humble servant. Yes, mentors are servants!

In summary, mentors help develop others into mature Christians and responsible leaders, and they lead by example.

Mentees

The mentees' role is to be prayerful, watchful, teachable and available. I cannot stress enough how important it is for mentees to have a teachable spirit. Mentees must have ears to hear and eyes and see – a vital message conveyed in Mark chapter 4. They must be ready to work actively and apply what has been taught or shown. The meanings of lessons they receive or observations they make may not be as clear as they would like – at first.

That's because learning is a process. For this reason, mentees should ask questions of God and mentors such as Samuel had done with Eli. The information, instruction, and training that mentees receive must enter their heart and not only their head. It's the difference between application and having information. This point is discussed in detail in my book, *Worship: Becoming What We See*. If such knowledge gets to the heart, mentees will be doers and not just hearers (James 1:22-25). It's within the best interest of mentees to pray for, respect, and bless their mentors.

Furthermore, mentees must observe, follow, and serve their mentors while exhibiting patience. I am placing emphasis on patience in the lives of mentees since they are apt to become eager, overzealous, and impatient as it pertains to the completion of their training stage, to become successors.

Mentoring Kingdom Style

Mentoring kingdom style has an adaptable method. In other words, mentors are clear about their role and communicates that role to their mentees. Even so, it is not a role or function that is specific to the mentor only but one that mentees must adapt – passing along to others what they have learned or have been taught. Mentees, too, are responsible for communicating what has been communicated to them.

Second Timothy 2:2 reads, *"The things [the doctrine, the precepts, the admonitions, the sum of my ministry] which you have heard me teach in the presence of many witnesses, entrust [as a treasure] to reliable and faithful men who will also be capable and qualified to teach others"* (AMP).

This letter is pastoral in nature, containing wise advice and a valuable lesson that can be applied to our lives and relationships, especially mantle anointing relationships – mentors should communicate to those who are faithful and can be trusted to do the same. They must be observant and selective in choosing others with whom to share.

Chapter 4: Time Awareness

Timing has its place in mantle anointing relationships – namely, God's timing. Time and timing have importance in such relationships when people are proactive about using them wisely; they add value to the process and proper development to those involved.

According to the American Dictionary of the English Language, the word *"time"* means *"To adapt to the time or occasion;* **to bring or perform at the proper season or time.***"* Time as we know it is constant, sure, fixed, and steady. Two things are eternal: God and time. Therefore, we should seek to understand the timeframe that God has allotted us and use it wisely, recognizing that opportunities come and go. In essence, Moses had this sentiment in his heart when he prayed, *"So teach us to number our days, that we may apply our hearts unto wisdom"* (Psalm 90:12, KJV). Time is valuable. We cannot afford to be unproductive with it.

Ecclesiastes 3:1 says, *"There is a time for everything, a season for every activity under heaven"* (NLT).

According to The Hebrew-Greek Key Study Bible, the word *"season"* is the Hebrew word *zeman*, which means *"an appointed occasion: season, time."* The word *"time"* is the Hebrew word *'eth*, which means *"[due] season."* Already we get the message that timing is crucial and that it has to do with a season or appointed occasion.

Timing also has to do with dispensations. A dispensation is a period of time that man is tested about obedience to some specific revelation of the will of God. Let us look further at the Bible's perspective as it relates to time and timing.

The phrase *"for such a time as this"* has become common language and a catchy cliché for Christians. Indeed, it has a nice ring to it, and we like to use it to convey messages on how God places us in positions at special times to accomplish specific tasks. But let us look more closely at this prophetic question posed to Esther by Mordecai, found in the book of Esther 4:14.

"If you keep quiet at a time like this, deliverance for the Jews will arise from some other place, but you and your relatives will die. What's more, who can say but that you have been elevated to the palace for just such a time as this?" (NLT).

Esther's elevation to the palace was a strategic move on God's part to bring deliverance to the Jews. Had Esther not seen herself as the vessel God would use in His timing, then she would have missed the opportunity of being used by God. God would then have to raise up someone else to do the work that He intended for Esther to do. Upon recognizing her opportunity and God's timing, Esther immediately sought God (Esther 4:16). She then combined courage with careful planning to carry out her mission. Courage alone was not enough for Esther to act upon. She knew that without a plan, she would not succeed! We sabotage ourselves, hindering and hampering our own production when we attempt to act without first consulting God and without devising a plan before moving forward.

Undoubtedly, God always has a purpose for placing us in various situations and environments. Esther could have given up hope, tried to save herself, or just waited around for God's intervention to come some other way. Instead, she recognized that God placed her in the palace for a specific purpose. Upon such recognition, she seized the moment and acted accordingly.

Moreover, she understood that had she not stepped up to help her people, God would send deliverance from elsewhere, and she and her father's house would not be spared. This teaches us a valuable lesson: we can sit in our safe, comfortable places while others suffer and are in dire need of help, but if we don't use our influence for the good of others, we can find ourselves in their shoes. The tables can quickly turn when selfishness and unwillingness take over.

In Romans 13:11, Paul talks about the importance of knowing what time it is. He says, *"Another reason for right living is that you know how late it is; time is running out. Wake up, for the coming of our salvation is nearer now than when we first believed"* (NLT). The King James Version of the Bible reads, *"...it is high time to awake out of sleep."* The words *"high time"* speak of a time favorable for seeking God. God's people must arise from inactivity and do the work of the Lord. Most people can reflect on wasted days, weeks, months, and years wishing they could get back wasted time, so they could do things differently. The reality is none of us can start over again. The best we can do is to start living wisely now. Wasted time cannot be redeemed. Since we know that God's timetable was established with a purpose for every person on this earth, we must ensure that we prepare and position ourselves so that God can call on us at any time.

Since God knows the beginning and end of all things, you and I must make sure that we know the mind of God by reading the Bible and through prayer, that we may operate in His divine will. Isaiah 55:8-9 tells us God's thoughts are not our thoughts and His ways are not our ways. Thus, we must seek to know and accept God's way of doing things.

The time for taking chances is over. When we are sure that God has called us to a specific purpose and has released us to accomplish *that* purpose, we should no longer waste time nor wait until we *feel* like moving forward to act upon that purpose. The Lord is coming soon. It's time to work while we have the knowledge of God's will! (John 9:4)

The question is: As Christians trying to work in God's timeframe, should we operate under God's permissive will or His divine will? I am confident in saying many of us operate under God's permissive will, meaning we do things that are not necessarily in the natural order of what God intends for our lives. God allows us to do those things because of our insensitivity to His divine will and, perhaps, because of our ignorance in knowing what the will of God is for our lives. Furthermore, our insistence can cause God to step back, allowing us to have our own way.

God will enable us to pursue that which brings pleasure to us, giving us over to our own selfish desires that we might be brought back to reconciliation with Him. God's intention in this allowance is not to grant us a license to sin – if sin is the issue – but, rather, to teach us valuable lessons from our mistakes that we may return to Him.

The working of God's permissive will unfolds in the same manner as parents relating to their children. Sometimes parents grant their children permission to do certain things, go to certain places, and give them what they want even though it may not be the best for them or the right time. They don't want such temptations for their children, but sometimes parents give in to the wishes of their children because of the constant asking and begging of the children. Reluctantly, parents give in.

At other times, parents may yield to their children's stubbornness and disobedience – especially as they become teenagers and young adults – knowing they are headed for regrets in life but can only pray for them that they will learn from their mistakes never to repeat them, but to become responsible, mature, and wise adults.

God is not passive. He *allows* us to do things and go places that are clearly out of the natural order of what He intended for our lives, reflecting the freedom of choice He has given us. Even though God nudges us – through the Holy Spirit – He allows us to go off track when we are determined to please ourselves more than pleasing Him. This permission is evident in the lives of God's people throughout the Bible and certainly in our lives and world today. When God nudges us, we should quickly and obediently respect His order, get back in line, and wait on His timing.

The Right Time

Galatians 4:4 reads,
"But when the right time came, God sent his Son, born of a woman, subject to the law" (NLT).
This verse refers to the prophecies about the coming of Christ and their fulfillment, showing us that when the fullness of time came for Jesus to enter this world, He did. The word *"fullness"* has to do with a specific time that applies to humanity since we live in time, and God lives in eternity.

"They will crush you to the ground, and your children with you. Your enemies will not leave a single stone in place, because you have rejected the opportunity God offered you" (Luke 19:44, NLT).

The word *"opportunity"* is the Greek translation of the word *"time."* When God gives us opportunities, we should take advantage of them. Otherwise, we may miss our divine visitation from God. In other words, at specific times or seasons of our lives, God makes His plan clear about what He expects of us and releases us to do those things, giving direction concerning the resources needed to accomplish the task. During these times, we should move forward without hesitation in what God urges us to do.

The best way to recognize the opportunities God gives us is through prayer, fasting, and study of the Bible. The more we draw near to God in relationship, the more He shows us His plan for our lives. Each plan has opportunities that will help us to fulfill God's purpose. He causes things to work on our behalf and others to favor us so that we can do His work. When we fail to recognize and move within God's timing, we miss the tremendous blessings of God at that moment. Moreover, we miss opportunities for growth and productivity.

Time and timing have to do with an occasion, a season, or a certain period of time; an opportunity. A pregnant woman does all she can to learn about the different trimesters of pregnancy, especially if it's her first pregnancy. She learns about what to expect during each trimester so that she can be knowledgeable and prepared concerning her condition. As she draws closer to the third trimester and the birth of her baby, she expects certain symptoms to be manifested or heightened. Feeling those symptoms prompts her to seek out the proper place or environment suitable for giving birth. In the same manner, we should be sensitive to our spiritual environment and condition so that as God deals with us in relation to timing and releasing us, we will be sensitive and aware of His movement. Don't miss God's timing!

Time awareness, then, can be best understood by looking at it as a birthing metaphor. We have to be aware of 'what time it is' by paying careful attention to signs around us and by getting in the right environment, which *may* be an inconvenience on our part. Those who know how God moves understands that – every now and then – He inconveniences us. Nevertheless, we must get in the place God wants us, so we can give birth – release – that which He has placed in us. Some of us would agree that we are more productive and achieve growth when we are challenged or placed in situations that inconvenience us. Challenges give us drive and determination to prove that we can grow beyond the challenge and overcome it.

In God-ordained mantle anointing relationships, we need to recognize God's timing. The story of Elijah and Elisha perfectly exemplifies timing. Elisha recognized that God had a plan for him and that His path would unfold each new step leading to that plan. This belief helped Elisha to take things as they came.

Chapter 5: Mantle Anointing Relationships ~ Moses & Joshua

Moses was born during a time when things were not going well for the Hebrew people, but the adversity he was born into did not interrupt God's purpose for his life, it solidified it. One of the methods God uses in preparing us for destiny is allowing us to encounter diverse experiences gained from a diverse background, such as Moses had (Acts 7:22). Moses was raised in royalty – Pharaoh's household (Exodus 2:10). Understanding Egyptian culture – their languages, beliefs, and customs – was necessary in relation to Moses' destiny. Moses had to be educated in Egyptian culture to prepare him for God's use later on as God would send him back into that environment to deliver His people – the Israelites. The emphasis is placed on the value of preparation.

Lessons

1. Application
As people of destiny, understanding what God teaches us through our experiences and learning how to apply those lessons in carrying out God's will are of utmost importance. Sometimes, however, we miss the connection between what life teaches us and how God wants us to use those lessons to accomplish His purpose in helping others.

God has a plan and purpose in every circumstance we face. Rather than trying to understand what that purpose is, we allow ourselves to be consumed and sidetracked by our adverse experiences – that which contradicts what God has said about us. Nevertheless, God can use adverse circumstances for our benefit. One of the ways God does so is by changing our perspective about what we face, causing us to commit everything into His care (Romans 8:28).

One day, as Moses worked in his occupation, he led the flock to what the King James Version of the Bible refers to as the *"back side of the desert"* – wilderness (Exodus 3:1). God led Moses to this wilderness place of solitude, so He could speak to him. God's intention was to share with Moses His plan and purpose for him. Although Moses did not expect to have an encounter with God, he was in the right place at the right time to hear from God. God had to lead him away from people to show him *His* glory. The angel of the Lord appeared to Moses in a flame of fire from a bush (Exodus 3:2). The bush was on fire, yet it wasn't consumed by the fire.

One can only imagine that the burning bush must have been a dramatic sight for Moses to see. God has a way of getting our attention! He knows what intrigues us. Moses said, *"I will now turn aside and see this great sight, why the bush does not burn"* (Exodus 3:3, NKJV). When God saw that he had gotten Moses' attention, He called to him, *"Moses! Moses!"*

The burning bush experience was the first time God spoke to Moses in this manner. Thus, God identified Himself as the One who knew those who were part of Moses' life and culture. God said, *"I am the God of your father, the God of Abraham, the God of Isaac, and the God of Jacob"* (Exodus 3:6, KJV). In essence, God was saying to Moses: I know your family, and I know where you come from. God understands human nature better than we do; He created us. Before He told Moses what He wanted him to do, he mentioned something that Moses could relate to, making him feel at ease.

2. Reluctance
When God shared with Moses the state of the children of Israel and how He wanted to use him to deliver them, Moses' reaction was, *"Who am I?"* (Exodus 3:7-11).

This response came because the task seemed greater than the one who was being asked to perform the task. Likewise, we tend to respond the same when God calls us to a task that we feel we cannot perform. Yet God would not *ask* us to do what He has not *enabled* and *equipped* us to do.

As Moses reluctantly tried to piece things together, he asked God, *"Who should I say sent me?"* In response to Moses' question, God revealed something about His character to Moses. God answered, *"I Am who I Am"* (Exodus 3:14, NLT). What a fantastic description of the God we serve! God is self-existent and all-sufficient. In other words, God made it clear to Moses that He does not rely on anyone else's strength or ability but, instead, everyone relies on His strength and power. God is omnipotent, omniscient, and omnipresent. The only name or title that God could give Moses to describe Himself was, *"I Am who I Am,"* which is God's name throughout generations and a memorial for all Christians (Exodus 3:15).

Memorials are linked to specific places designated to offering sacrifices unto God – a common practice throughout the Old Testament. The act of memorializing was instituted and performed whenever God delivered His people out of a bad situation. In Joshua's case, for example, the children of Israel walked across the Jordan River and set up stones as a memorial that God had brought them across the river. Memorials are those things that help us to preserve the memory of experiences we encounter and, most importantly, to preserve the memory of how God brought us through those particular experiences.

Moses had many experiences to 'memorialize' as it was God's power alone that helped him lead Israel out of Egypt, and that was just part of his God-ordained purpose. Moses had more experiences than he bargained for, and more than he was able to manage in his own strength.

Nevertheless, Moses began his journey towards accomplishing his God-given purpose in life (Exodus chapters 4 through 11). Moses was called to deliver Israel from Pharaoh's rule and to mentor others, one of whom God would choose to someday succeed him. In addition to being called as Israel's ruler and deliverer, Moses was used by God to lead Israel into an experience of God's redemption, as is reflected throughout the book of Exodus. (See Acts 7:35).

3. Faith and Perseverance
Although God used many plagues and signs – through Moses – against the Egyptians to soften Pharaoh's heart to release Israel, their freedom did not come right away. God was teaching Moses a lesson of faith, trust, and perseverance. The Greek translation of the word *"perseverance"* is *"hupomone"* – perseverance coupled with patience and endurance. Letting go of faith is easy to do when things don't look like they are lining up the way God said they would, but God is true to His word, and He will deliver! We must persevere in spite of challenges.

The Release and the Departure

When God moved upon Pharaoh's heart to release Israel (the tenth plague, Exodus 12:29-30), Moses was already a great man in the land of Egypt, in the sight of Pharaoh's servants, and in the sight of the people (Exodus 11:3). Every challenge, obstacle, and rejection that Moses faced contributed to his greatness in God. Moses had many opportunities to strengthen his faith in God, just as we do today.

4. Signs of Defeat
Moses had many opportunities to flex his spiritual muscles in the face of what seemed to be defeat. Signs of defeat may be all around us, yet God can step in the midst of what appears to be a losing battle, turn things around to work out on our behalf, giving us the victory.

5. God, our Champion
From a human standpoint, Moses felt like he was fighting a losing battle, but God was on his side. He enabled Moses to lead the children of Israel out of Egypt through the Red Sea Crossing (Exodus 13:17 to 14:16-29). God will bring darkness and destruction to those circumstances that try to defeat us just as He did for Moses (Exodus 14:19-20).

God continued to use Moses mightily after the Exodus and the Red Sea Crossing. By now, Moses was considered a friend of God, and God talked with him. When Moses looked for the comfort of knowing who would accompany him in tasks he had to accomplish and things he had to face in the future, God told him that His Presence would be with him much like a companion (Exodus 33:14).

6. Experiences
Moses' experiences were not for his benefit alone, but to prepare him to train his successor, Joshua. In Moses' role as a mentor, he first had to learn how to trust and obey God. Life can be miserable for the Christian who refuses to trust God, going in the opposite direction of God's intended purpose.

7. The Minority
Moses questioned God about various aspects of his tasks either because he saw no logic in what God was asking him to do, he doubted God, or he feared that the people would not understand the things he did or show him respect. Mentors may not *always* gain understanding from others, nor will they *always* be supported by the majority. Lack of support from the majority – those who carry weight, the influencers who represent the majority – causes some to interpret this to mean that the mentor is not called, appointed, or anointed. At times, we question whether we're in God's will based on how others receive and perceive us.

As a mentor, Moses had to learn to rely on God entirely. In order to effectively lead others, He had to follow his Mentor – God. An important aspect about mentors is their ability and willingness as followers prior to mentoring others, as this helps to prepare them to lead. Joshua – the mentee – had to see firsthand Moses' obedience in following God's instructions.

Joshua

Who was Joshua, and why did God choose him to succeed Moses? What qualified him for the job? Joshua was the son of Nun and Moses' servant or minister. According to the New Living Translation of the Bible, Numbers 11:28 tells us that Joshua was Moses' personal assistant since his youth. Obviously, a close-knit relationship existed between Moses and Joshua early in Joshua's life.

8. Observation
Joshua had many opportunities to observe Moses while he faced every challenge and obstacle in trying to do the will of God, which teaches us something important: mentors can't train others, be an example to them and – at the same time – keep a personal or private profile. Openness and willingness to share on the part of the mentor is required in establishing an authentic, down-to-earth relationship with the mentee. That which contributes to the overall development of mentees are opportunities for observing their mentor in action, not just the positive aspect of their mentor's work, but the challenging ones too.

9. Privileges of the Mentee [Successor]
Joshua received a charge from God to stand in place of Moses (Joshua 1:1-5). In fact, the Israelites first entered Canaan under Joshua's rule (Joshua 1:1-5:12).

Thus, Joshua's specific role was to lead Israel into victory over their circumstances. Consequently, this stage of Joshua's ministry could not occur until the Israelites were brought back to God – redeemed and re-focused – which was Moses' role. Thus, we see how important it is for mentors and mentees to know their role and operate therein.

God may give the mentor a vision of what He wants to bring to pass, but for various reasons may not allow the mentor to carry out the vision. God may allow the mentee to bring the vision to fruition. This was the case with Joshua leading Israel into Canaan – The Promised Land. In other words, leaders get the vision, but they may not be the ones to carry it out.

There needs to be concern about leaders who don't train others for succession nor share information to prepare others to step into more significant roles. This applies to prospective successors and those who are already leaders serving under pastors who – unfortunately – don't invest in them, share valuable information with them, or train them to be better leaders.

An important observation is that the successor – catcher of the mantle – may be chosen to do things that his or her predecessor *could not* or *was not permitted* to do. For example, Moses could not lead the children of Israel into Canaan because of his disobedience as a result of unbelief. Let's look at the story briefly.

The children of Israel complained because they had no water to drink, and they spoke against Moses and Aaron (Numbers 20:1-5). Moses and Aaron then sought God through prayer for guidance on how to handle the disgruntled Israelites. God instructed Moses and Aaron to speak to the rock, and the rock would, in turn, produce water (Numbers 20:6-8). Moses and Aaron did not follow God's instructions.

On the contrary, they smote the rock twice with the rod instead of speaking to it (Numbers 20:11). This action was a sign of unbelief on Moses' part because he was the leader, not Aaron. Perhaps Moses became comfortable using the rod to work miracles and did not believe that actually speaking to a rock would produce a miracle.

10. Anger
Moses was angry with the children of Israel and referred to them as rebels in Numbers 20:10. His anger could have obstructed his focus from doing what God asked him to do. Moses' behavior is a lesson to us that we should not act or respond out of anger. Anger expressed in the wrong way causes us to do or say the wrong things (Ephesians 4:26).

  Because Moses disobeyed God out of unbelief, he was not allowed to enter the Promise Land of Canaan (Numbers 20:12). Joshua, on the other hand, was permitted to enter Canaan.

  Joshua was qualified to succeed Moses in becoming Israel's leader for a number of reasons. First, God appointed him, and that was a qualifier all by itself (Numbers 27:18-23). Second, he was one of the only two living eyewitnesses to the Egyptian plagues and the Exodus from Egypt. Joshua had seniority; he had been around for a while and endured with Moses and the children of Israel through good and bad times.

  Joshua's longsuffering and patience showed that he was dependable and a stable force before God elevated him. Third, he was Moses' personal assistant for forty years. In Joshua's life, we see stability, consistency, reliability, dependability, and loyalty. Fourth, of the twelve scouts Moses sent out to spy the land of Canaan, Joshua and Caleb were the only two who showed complete confidence that God would help them conquer the land. Joshua was well prepared to lead the nation of Israel.

11. Changes in Leadership

A change in leadership was necessary in order for the nation of Israel to move to the place that God intended them to be. Joshua was fit for leadership because he had been tested and was faithful to God's leader, Moses. Quite naturally, Joshua was affected by the adversity encountered as a result of walking with God's leader, but he was not shaken in his faith. He was the man for the job. Thus, the only approval necessary for Joshua to be the next leader of Israel was God's approval.

When changes in leadership occur, it's vital that certain things transpire on the part of the individual leaving a particular position; thereby, ensuring a smooth transition for the establishment and arrival of the new administration. A smooth transition can't occur unless aspiring leaders are adequately trained and those currently in leadership have done a job well, so that their successors can enter the position not being ill equipped. Current leaders should be preparing others, by God's leading, to take their place so that when they leave a position or are promoted, operations can continue to run smoothly, effectively, and efficiently. Joshua's job consisted of leading the nation of Israel into a new land and conquering that land. Of course, Joshua had his moments of fear and doubt. In fact, such insecurity caused God to encourage Joshua on many occasions, telling him to be strong and courageous and not to be afraid or discouraged.

New jobs present tremendous opportunities to showcase one's skillset, but they also present challenges that can produce doubt and fear in those assigned to the task, especially if they are unprepared and untrained. Joshua's success depended on his obedience to the law Moses gave and faith in God (Joshua 1:7-8).

While Moses was in leadership, he knew he would not hold the position forever and that one day someone would succeed him. There is a beginning and an ending to everything.

That's why it's important that we make every second count for God and use the time He has given us wisely.

      Mentors must recognize when it's time to pass the baton to their mentee, depending on the work at hand. By the same token, mentees should value the time spent with their mentor, recognizing that one day they may occupy that position or a similar one.

12. Stability

Once again, Joshua served Moses for forty years. This speaks of longevity and stability. He had been tested – 40 is the number of testing – and was proven capable. He was consistently in Moses' presence to observe, learn, and assist. The very nature of the word *"served"* implies that Joshua had something to offer Moses. He assisted Moses well. He recognized when Moses was tired and weak and stepped in to help him win battles. (See Exodus 17:12).

      Not all mentees are as fortunate as Joshua was to be around his predecessor for that length of time. Even so, if God establishes such a relationship, then whatever time is allotted for the mentor and mentee to work together is sufficient and should be used wisely. Proper time management ensures a healthy, profitable exchange of that which is needed to develop a relationship, preparing *both* individuals for the transition.

13. Faith

One of the reasons Joshua was chosen as Moses' successor was because of his faith in God. Joshua's faith was exemplified in God's ability to lead Israel into Canaan (Numbers 14:6-9; 13:30-33).

God wants our complete trust and faith to be placed in Him! Faith will get the job done when nothing else can.

If this book has blessed you in any way, kindly leave a professional, positive review on Amazon.com ~ thank you!

Chapter 6: Mantle Anointing Relationships ~ Jesus & His Disciples

Jesus Christ was in a mantle anointing relationship with the twelve disciples during His earthly ministry. The disciples spent a lot of time with Jesus being taught by Him and observing what He did. The New Testament book of Matthew 10:1-2; 4:18-22; 9:9 lists the names of the twelve apostles. The words *"apostles"* and *"disciples"* are used interchangeably.

Lessons

1. Teaching and Observation

Teaching and observation are vitally important to the one catching the mantle – the mentee. Instruction helps to ensure the mentee receives a well-balanced flow of information and is able to process such information in ways that are useful, contributes to his or her overall growth, and prepares him or her for the role of a successor.

Teaching is principal to having well-balanced mantle anointing relationships. It embodies training; they go hand-in-hand. Furthermore, teaching provides the foundation to such relationships testing durability and effectiveness as it relates to carrying out the mission.

"And he [Jesus] appointed twelve, that they might be with Him and that He might send them out to preach..." (Mark 3:14, KJV; brackets added).

The words *"be with him"* in Mark 3:14 imply keeping company with, associating with, or being in the same sphere with. Jesus had an inner circle of men whom He groomed, taught, and trained to carry on the work of the Father.

I use the term *"inner circle"* to emphasize the fact that the disciples were 'called' by Jesus to follow Him – not that they initially wanted to on their own or planned to. They were challenged to leave their earthly work to learn of Him. This is very different than cliques of today that isolate people, making them feel unimportant and unwanted. The mission and purpose of Christ could not be entrusted to those who had never been in close relationship with Him or trained by Him (Luke 4:43). Surely to whom much was given, much was required (Luke 12:48). His selection process of the disciples does not portray Him as disassociating with others. On the contrary, more than associating with others, He extended grace to all He came in contact with, including those with whom the religious leaders would not associate (Mark 2:13-17).

When it came down to sharing His mission intimately and equipping others to work in cooperation with Him, Jesus groomed a select few – initially – but throughout His ministry, the number of disciples grew.

In the New Testament book of Mark 3:13-15, we learn that the apostles were ordained to be with Jesus as well as to be sent out by Him to preach, heal, and cast out devils.

2. Competitiveness
In their daily travel with Jesus, the disciples asked Him questions about everything and rightfully so since they were in training. They asked Him questions about what He did and why He did it. Their minds were curious about the One they served. They asked Jesus trivial, selfish questions like who would be the greatest in the kingdom? In mantle anointing relationships involving more than one mentee, competitiveness can stick its neck up because each mentee wants to feel closer to the mentor as if that qualifies him or her for the greatest role.

Jesus experienced the carnality and pettiness of His disciples as a result of their mindset. Jesus – the Mentor – always steered the disciples to what was most important. He re-trained their mind to think as He did. The Bible teaches that carnal thinking is an enemy of God (Romans 8:7). That's why the Lord trained His disciples to think about spiritual things and outcomes. (See Philippians 3). The matter of carnality is one of the reasons the scripture admonishes us, *"Let this mind be in you, which was also in Christ Jesus"* (Philippians 2:5, KJV). This verse really deals with submission. The disciples had to learn to submit to the Lord and to each other. Submission is necessary as someone has to lead, and someone has to submit to leadership. While Jesus was with the disciples, He kept them focused so that they could understand the seriousness of the work they were being trained for.

3. The Test

During the time Jesus spent with His disciples, He tested them to see how well they knew Him. For example, He asked them in Matthew 16:15-16, *"...But whom say ye that I am? And Simon Peter answered and said, Thou art the Christ, the Son of the living God"* (KJV). Following Peter's confession, Jesus shared more in-depth with them concerning His future impending suffering and death. The time had come in their relationship for Jesus to share on this level.

It was a time of vulnerability for the Mentor as He entrusted them with sensitive, weighty information. The same rule applies to mantle anointing relationships. Mentors don't share everything in the beginning stages of the relationship – prematurely. The reason being mentees must be tested along the way concerning their commitment to the relationship, devotion to God, and loyalty to their mentor. Additionally, mentees may not be ready – mature enough – to handle confidential information. Peter's confession of Jesus being *the Christ, Son of the living God,* was proof that he was in tune with the Father. He received divine revelation.

4. Channeling Desire
Not everyone has been fitted for a person-to-person mantle anointing relationship, yet some desire to be involved in such a relationship. Desire, in and of itself, is not a bad thing, but there needs to be an understanding that just because an individual desires it doesn't mean he or she will – or should – have it.

Knowing God hasn't paired you in a mantle anointing relationship – as a mentor or mentee – is reason enough not to pursue that kind of relationship. Insisting on doing so, whether for status or friendship, will only cause turmoil, confusion, and frustration. Frankly, the relationship will not last. A mantle anointing relationship is not the same as a friendship. Some people confuse the two.

I have personally experienced frustration in trying to mentor individuals who approached me to be mentored but weren't truly ready. In those cases, the mentoring never lasted long and always ended abruptly. Perhaps they wanted something else like a friendship. Maybe they wanted to be mentored their own way – in a manner comfortable for them. I have learned when a mentoring relationship is not meant to be, to let it go. One hundred percent of the times, the individual wanting to be mentored won't stick to or complete assignments.

Sometimes people see an individual they admire, aspire to be like, or are inspired by. Because of that, they feel a mentoring relationship would be ideal but that's not necessarily true. Listen, there has to be a calling to the same or a similar purpose in a mentoring relationship. There has to be a fit. For this reason, I no longer mentor individuals simply because they ask me to.

I can look back on a time when I mentored an individual who sought after me and truly desired to be mentored. In this case, there was good success on both sides.

Initially, I don't think she knew all that was involved, but her heart was in it for the right reasons. I was able to pour into her without holding back – challenge her and give her assignments that helped shape her personally and spiritually. Not only was it a mentoring relationship, she also served me in different capacities – accompanying me on speaking engagements, covering me in prayer, blessing me as she saw a need or even a desire, and walking with me through a season of great trial in my life. She was a true mentee as I was a true mentor. That season of mentoring, which lasted approximately three years – until she relocated to another state – established a firm foundation and a solid relationship between us that exists to this day. We are friends.

To mentor and be mentored employs our desires, which should be channeled toward God, so they don't lead us into that which displeases Him or is out of His will. Our desires are wrongful when we insist on stepping out of God's will to pursue what we want; that's where trouble begins. Furthermore, timing may be an issue. In other words, stepping out of God's time to do or gain something – by default – puts us out of His will. When we rally for things to happen, knowing God has not sanctioned them, we experience confusion, un-preparedness, and the pain and consequences of our premature actions.

5. Attraction
A special attraction occurs between individuals selected for mantle anointing relationships prior to the actual pairing up. Sometimes the attraction happens casually and – seemingly – unintentionally; thus, you may not recognize it as being more than an ordinary relationship. But as time goes on, you begin to identify more specifically with an individual and with what God is doing in that person's life. As you spend more time with the individual, you can combine your efforts to accomplish the same purpose.

Certain signs could mean that you are being fitted for a mantle anointing relationship. The answer can certainly be obtained through prayer.

The attraction that occurs in mantle anointing relationships encompasses a drawing together physically, spiritually, emotionally, and mentally. In other words, everything works together, creating a bond between those involved – a genuine interest forms between the individuals and the work involved, including identifiable characteristics that God can accentuate in the relationship and the work.

The best way I can describe such an attraction is by saying it's magnetic. With this kind of attraction, mentees know they are connected to their mentor in *some* way and that the connection is more than just admiring someone. For instance, mentees can identify with the mission, goals, purpose, and destiny of their mentor. Moreover, mentees can recognize similarities in the work style and execution methods of their mentor.

Those in mantle anointing relationships may not have the opportunity to thoroughly know each other or work together for an extended length of time prior to being paired together. The pairing may happen spontaneously and suddenly without clear indications; yet those involved will know it is of God.

One of the key aspects of a mantle anointing relationship is the 'catcher's' ability to do what he or she sees the 'thrower' doing without deviating from it. Thus, catchers must be willing to follow and submit. Throwers, on the other hand, must demonstrate the ability to properly train and 'pass the torch' to their catcher or successor. In modern days – generally speaking – there are churches that have either abandoned the concept of mantle anointing relationships, or they never embraced it to begin with.

Consequently, throwers who fill key roles but will eventually move on to other roles, fail to identify and train potential successors to fill those roles.

All too often, throwers are not fostering, grooming, or equipping catchers to do what they have done and more than they have done. Thus, as they move on to other roles and tasks, a vacancy or void is left in the particular position they once filled. In this state of un-preparedness, we find – often through frustration – a state of unreadiness and unwillingness as it pertains to the local church in filling vacancies, which circles back to lack of training others. Moreover, such lack can result from throwers feeling insecure about letting go.

We need to be reminded that we are stewards. We don't own anything. We must be mindful that *God* qualifies and calls us to roles, positions, and tasks. That means we are at *His* disposal. At any time, God can shift us from one position to another, and our responsibility is to cooperate with Him. The Bible clearly teaches that promotion comes from God, which should eliminate the feeling or need for being possessive or territorial over our *little* positions (Psalm 75:6-7). When a person tries to do everything himself or herself – neglecting to train or delegate when there is a need to – it may be an indication of several things – he or she is insecure, ignorant, does not trust others, or, perhaps, does not know how to train or delegate.

6. Recognition
Recognizing the abilities of others is vital in establishing mantle anointing relationships, especially on the part of the thrower.
As a leader, Jesus knew each of His disciples' abilities, both naturally and spiritually.

In organizations, when an individual's given too much responsibility and little to no training, it can result in losses to the department, organization, and even loss of that person's job.
Training is essential and most beneficial in equipping others to do the best job they can, especially in positions of leadership. Jesus trained His disciples. He didn't just work with them for a month and then send them out to serve others. He consistently and regularly worked with them before releasing them to go out on their own (Matthew 10:1-20).

With regards to the five-fold ministry-gifts in Ephesians 4:11-13, there are those who feel that –because there is little time left in terms of Jesus' return for the church – individuals should be rushed along in these ministry-gifts, so they can be released to use them. But to whose detriment? It's a fact that Jesus is coming soon for His bride – the church without spot or wrinkle or any such thing – but that doesn't mean sacrificing preparedness for being gifted. Doing so is a recipe for disaster if an individual is not mature in his or her gifting and grounded in the Lord.

Let me be more transparent. *Some* believe and practice that a person can get saved today and – without any preparation, testing, or process at all – go out and preach tomorrow, for example, because time is running out and the gospel must be preached to all the world. Let me explain so that you won't misunderstand what I'm saying. Sharing your testimony or a scripture with others is not the same as the ministry gift of preaching, which requires skill, knowledge of the Bible, a surrendered life, and so much more. Indeed, the gospel must be preached to all the world. But there are those whom God has called to do so. If you're one of them, thank God for you. Preach well! All regenerated Christian believers are required to share what they know about Christ with those who are lost in sin, but such sharing isn't to be confused with preaching the gospel.

Training is a salient part of our continual growth and maturity concerning the things of God. Only then, can discipleship, in its proper form, occur.

The act of pursuing differs from person to person, depending on what or whom is being sought, the pursuer's interest, level of maturity, experience, and knowledge base. I recommend prayerful pursuit with regards to the five-fold ministry-gifts and the spiritual gifts the Lord has given to members of His body. (I Corinthians 12, 14; Romans 12:3-8, Ephesians 4:11-16).

The endowment of the five-fold ministry-gifts comes to those who are 'called.' The call comes from God, which means He has carte blanche in the preparation process. We can quickly get into trouble failing to recognize that there is *always* a process and season of preparation for any calling that God places upon us, not allowing that process to run its divine course in our lives. We should not be eager to ship people off – or be shipped off ourselves – as soon as they say there's a call on their life, even if it's evident to others, especially new babes in Christ or spiritually immature Christians who have been in the church for years. An exception would be those who are mature in Christ, have been faithful in serving Him and their local church, who walk in obedience and have already been functioning in their calling informally.

Spiritual maturity, a life surrendered and submitted to Christ, and the ability to rightly divide the word of truth shouldn't be optional. It's possible for an individual to be gifted yet lack all of these things. That's why preparation and training are necessary. Furthermore, there is nothing wrong with testing an individual to see where he or she stands in terms of commitment to God and the 'call' itself before releasing him or her. Personal and spiritual development and training takes time; they don't happen overnight.

The production of God's mission on the part of the church should not be handled using the same methods as the world; for example, the concept of fast-food chains. Their goal is to get people in, served, and out as quickly as possible with little waiting, whether standing in line or ordering from the comfort of their vehicle. Notice, most fast-food chains don't serve the most nutritional foods. Think about that, and then translate it into the spiritual. Do you get my point?

7. Motive
Mentees should be careful of their motive in terms of what draws them to mentors. The attraction shouldn't be based on popularity, title, fame, wealth, position, accomplishments or the like. The attraction should be godly for the sole purpose of continuing God's work here on earth so that mentors can move on to the next task God has for them.

In addition, mentees should not desire to be in a mantle anointing relationship simply because they covet – in a selfish, fleshly manner – the anointing they may witness in the lives of mentors. The anointing is costly! Mentees should know this if they don't already. There is a cost to be paid to function under the anointing of the Holy Spirit accomplishing great things for the Lord. God doesn't endow anyone without first testing and proving that person, and He often does so throughout one's lifetime (II Corinthians 12:7-10).

Operating under a great anointing also costs in terms of self-sacrificing. Those who are not willing to pay the price to walk in the anointing of God should not covet the anointing of another. They should be content with what they have.

8. The Servant's Profile
Until mentees become successors of their mentors, they should continue serving or ministering to their mentors.

A person's unwillingness to serve and follow will affect his or her ability to lead effectively. Right attitudes need to be established before mentees become mentors.

Great leaders are made out of humble servants, and there is a level of contentment that comes with being a servant. In other words, an individual should serve with joy even though he or she may know that God has bigger – and perhaps better – things in store for him or her. This doesn't mean that being a servant is insignificant or unimportant. In fact, the opposite is true – only people with character and integrity can genuinely serve others. There's no insignificance in that.

Patience and humility are attributes needed in servants. This is where contentment comes into play – contentment in being a servant. David was anointed king over Israel around the age of sixteen but he didn't fill that office until around the age of thirty. God had a great call on Moses' life but didn't communicate that to Moses until he was well into his adulthood on the backside of the desert (Acts 7:23-24, 29-30). Elisha humbly served Elijah until it was his time to become Elijah's successor.

A glimpse of Bible characters throughout this book shows us their characteristics. No doubt they possessed what we have come to know as the fruit of the Spirit. You may say that's impossible since Jesus Christ had not yet been born, crucified and resurrected, and the Holy Spirit had not yet been given. On the contrary, it is possible – maybe in different terms – as the Holy Spirit moved throughout the Old Testament. Remember, the Old Testament was a shadow of things to come – the New Testament or New Covenant. Jesus' earthly ministry defined that which was evident in the lives of godly Old Testament leaders.

The principles shared in this section are chief. They give us knowledge about lessons God wants us to learn. Furthermore, they teach us how to apply the knowledge we receive so we can be well balanced and better equipped to accomplish God's purposes.

Chapter 7: Mantle Anointing Relationships ~ Paul & Timothy

Following Paul's conversion to Christianity and undergoing a process prior to the Lord sending him back to the same city and the ones he sought to persecute, he became a spiritual father to many, Timothy being one. Paul's writings of the Epistles were Spirit-led. There's no doubt in my mind that the zeal Paul – then Saul – had in persecuting the church was unmatched to his passion as a Christian believer, an apostle, and a missionary.

I often wonder whether Paul underwent great trials and persecution as a Christian believer because of the persecution he brought upon Christians prior to his conversion. We know that God is forgiving, but there are times when wrongful actions can bring about consequences even after seeking God's forgiveness. We can be sorry for what we have done or said, but in some cases, we still must suffer the consequences.

As a new convert to Christianity, persecution was inevitable. Paul became a magnet for the attacks of the devil through religious leaders and others because of his stance for Jesus Christ and the gospel message he taught and preached.

The Lord used Paul to write one-third of the New Testament books, which have lasting eternal value and substantial spiritual impact. Looking through the lens of Paul, he took his own identity as a Christian believer solemnly. He was devoted to the Lord and His gospel message. Paul didn't allow people's opinions of him to sway, deter, or stop him from doing the work of the Lord. He was all in, no matter the cost. Even while imprisoned, he wrote letters to the churches known as prison epistles. Indeed, his life exemplified the truth of the scripture that reads, *"Wherein I suffer trouble, as an evil doer, even unto bonds; but the word of God is not bound.*

Therefore, I endure all things for the elect's sakes that they may also obtain the salvation which is in Christ Jesus with eternal glory." (II Timothy 2:9-10).

Who better to father Timothy than Paul? While on his second missionary journey, Paul met Timothy, who became his companion and co-worker along with Silas. *"Paul went first to Derbe and then to Lystra, where there was a young disciple named Timothy. His mother was a Jewish believer, but his father was a Greek. Timothy was well thought of by the believers in Lystra and Iconium, so Paul wanted him to join them on their journey. In deference to the Jews of the area, he arranged for Timothy to be circumcised before they left, for everyone knew that his father was a Greek. Then they went from town to town, instructing the believers to follow the decisions made by the apostles and elders in Jerusalem. So, the churches were strengthened in their faith and grew larger every day"* (Acts 16:1-5, NLT). Here began the loving mentoring relationship between Paul and Timothy. Note the word *"loving."* There can be no mentoring outside of love, for it is love – more accurately, the love of God in us – that causes mentors to pour themselves unselfishly into mentees without reservation. Furthermore, love activates a patience in mentors to wait on mentees as they grow, further develop, and choose to go all the way with the relationship and all that it offers.

Paul's letters to Timothy had specific purposes. Let's look at what they are. In the book of First Timothy, Paul admonishes Timothy as a son to shun false teachings and to cling to his faith in Christ and keep his conscience clear. Paul instructs Timothy about worship – prayer, intercession, thanksgiving, and lifting holy hands to God.

Additionally, Paul goes into great detail describing the qualities church leaders should exemplify – namely bishops and deacons – such as faithfulness in marriage – including managing their own household well, having children who respect and obey them – self-control, wise living, a good reputation, enjoying hospitality, not be a drunkard or violent, but gentle – one who is spoken well of. For the role of deacons, Paul adds that they must have integrity and not be dishonest with money, but committed to the faith, living with a clear conscience.

In the book of II Timothy, Paul tells Timothy what to teach others, such as discerning false teachings, the deceitfulness of riches and the temptation they bring, and wandering from faith in Christ. Furthermore, Paul emphasizes the blessing of having and knowing what true riches are – true godliness with contentment, which is itself great wealth. Paul gives final instructions to Timothy while also affirming him as a man of God.

The thrower – Paul – tells the catcher – Timothy – to run from all these evil things and to pursue righteousness and a godly life, along with faith, love, perseverance, and gentleness (I Timothy 6:11-12). Paul's instructions and warnings to Timothy were always in-depth and thorough. He doesn't just tell Timothy what to flee. He goes on to tell him what to pursue. As a mentor, it was Paul's responsibility to drive the message home. That's what mentors do. They don't let up. They leave no room for guessing on the part of the mentee. In so doing, they help to anchor the truth into the soul of mentees.

Paul held Timothy accountable for what he taught him. That's what good throwers do. He issued a charge to Timothy before the Almighty God to obey his commandment without wavering. Paul knew that if Timothy did this, no one could find fault with him.

Timothy had done well declaring to countless others the eternal life that God called him to – life that can be obtained only through Jesus Christ.

As a mentor, Paul knew just when to encourage Timothy and provide instruction. This could not occur apart from the closeness they shared – the mantle anointing relationship. In one instance, Paul urged Timothy to be faithful as a good soldier of Jesus Christ.

Paul's role as a mentor was also to remind Timothy of good and necessary practices. In another instance, he reminded Timothy to fan into flames the gift of God that was in him by the laying on of his [Paul's] own hands (II Timothy 1:6-7).
This reminder resulted from Paul himself remembering Timothy's genuine faith and background.

This leads me to something else. The laying on of hands is not to be taken or done lightly. It is a sacred act. The mentor who lays hands on his or her mentee – *if* and *when* it is required – must ensure that the mentee's in right standing with God and others, as he or she – the mentor – must also be. For example, Paul modeled before Timothy, taught, and mentored him to live above reproach. That way, no one could blame Timothy for living an ungodly or hypocritical life as a man of God. He practiced what he preached to others. Moreover, Timothy was devoted to Christ and His gospel message as a faithful servant. He wasn't one who lived any kind of life while calling himself a Christian believer and church leader. This made Timothy an ideal candidate for the laying on of Paul's hands but also to – himself – lay hands on others. He had been proven and was qualified.

Paul admonished Timothy to never be in a hurry to lay hands on others (I Timothy 5:22-24). This addresses the matter of ordination and appointment of church leaders.

It's not difficult to understand why Paul admonished Timothy in this way. In their days – as well as today – there were those who had a different agenda than that of Jesus Christ and the gospel message. They were impure, leading believers astray – the false teachers Paul talks about.

The spiritual and ministry gift of teaching is a venue through which Satan infiltrates the church. Paul warns Timothy against false teachings in I Timothy 1 and speaks of those having 'itching ears' in II Timothy 4:3. You see, Satan's tactic is to always distort and falsify the truth. He entices individuals by presenting a little truth upfront to lure them, and before you know it, he has them in his clutch. For some, by the time they realize they've been fed a bunch of lies, it's too late because they've already departed from the truth of God's Word and His will.

Paul was an ideal thrower to Timothy – and others. In summary, Paul covered all areas that were crucial to Timothy's success as a church leader, that he would remain grounded in Jesus Christ, be steadfast in the gospel message in the face of false teachers and evil doers and be a humble servant-leader – one who prays for others, teaching them the gospel truth.

Chapter 8: Male to Female Mantle Anointing Relationships

If it must be so, male to female mantle anointing relationships must have some precautions. First, those involved in this kind of relationship should ensure that there's no physical attraction – that the desire to connect is not a crush or infatuation. When it comes to opposite sexes, mistaking attraction for mantle anointing relationships can happen. Boundaries must be established and honored in terms of how closely the two work together, the setting in which they work, and the circumstances surrounding their work. Going on right motives alone is not enough. You can be morally strong until you continually put yourself in positions to be otherwise. Let's be real; temptation is temptation. Many people have yielded to temptation when they had not set out with that in mind.

In the late '90s, I was asked by a brother in the Lord to mentor him. At the time, we attended the same church. I get it; he saw me as someone he could learn a lot from in a particular area. Notwithstanding, however, I didn't think that it would be a wise move on my part, so I didn't mentor him. For me, it wasn't about temptation as much as the possibility of others misinterpreting the relationship. I explained my decision to the brother although I didn't have to. In mantle anointing relationships, I personally believe that men should mentor men and women should mentor women. That's what I believe, and that's what I practice. Moreover, Romans 14:16 says, *"Therefore do not let what you know is good be spoken of as evil"* (NIV). The one exception is an older or more mature couple (husband and wife) mentoring a younger man or woman. In this case, the mentoring should be done as a couple.

If a male mentee is scheduled for mentoring on a given day but something comes up and the male mentor becomes unavailable to provide mentoring alongside his wife, then they should reschedule for a day they both can mentor the gentleman together.

At the onset of Romans 14, Paul addresses those who are weak in faith versus those who are strong in faith. He doesn't do so to judge either side, but rather to teach – and correct – by making clear points on the subject of food and sacred days. The message is that God accepts everyone. Just because you believe that something is right to do or practice doesn't mean it will be interpreted as right or good to the one who is weaker in faith.
Let me be clear; the message here is not concerning doctrine or salvation. These are entirely different than what Paul addresses. Those who know the Lord, must obey His teachings in the Bible.

A closeness forms in mantle anointing relationships, which means walls come down and people open up to each other. Sometimes the sharing goes beyond the focus area for mentoring. It goes without saying that throwers and catchers should do all they can to ensure they don't let down the wrong wall since everyone has areas of vulnerability. Sharing inappropriately increases the likelihood of vulnerability, being tempted and yielding. There are areas that should be off-limits – whether for sharing, discussion, observance, or participation. Neither the thrower nor the catcher should empower the other person with more information than he or she needs to know. Not everyone can handle openness, transparency, and honesty about certain aspects of one's life. In some cases, if an individual reads into it as being an area of weakness or as the other person being needy, that increases the likelihood of the relationship going where it was not designed to. Openness can be used as a tool of empowerment and abuse in the hands of the wrong person. For example, dependency that's both unhealthy and unholy can occur.

There is a need for both the thrower and catcher to examine whether God has paired them or something else is at work. Moreover, loneliness must be channeled properly in throwers and catchers alike – both single *and* married.

Chapter 9: Modern-day Mantle Anointing Relationships

In the previous chapter, I addressed male to female mantle anointing relationships. In this chapter, I will give an example of such a relationship before moving on to others.

The first example is Evangelist Kathryn Kuhlman and Evangelist Benny Hinn. Your goal should be to hear what God *may* want to say to you through this chapter more than focusing on the individuals that are used as examples. Kathryn Kuhlman was an American Evangelist whose ministry focused on healing services. Benny Hinn is an Israeli televangelist and evangelist known for his miracle crusades – revivals and faith healing summits. He wears the mantle anointing of Kathryn Kuhlman. In fact, he shares about the miracles he witnessed and experienced as he attended Evangelist Kuhlman's conferences. These experiences came about shortly after he accepted the Lord Jesus Christ as his Savior as a teenager. (See *Good Morning, Holy Spirit* by Benny Hinn). To say these experiences were life-changing for him is an understatement. There was a greater call on Evangelist Hinn's life, and it was necessary for him to encounter Evangelist Kuhlman.

Evangelist Kuhlman was known as the woman who believed in miracles. What Evangelist Hinn witnessed in her ministry drove him closer to God, seeking God for the same demonstration of power in his life. He wanted God's power – the inner working of the Holy Spirit – to be as real in his life as He was in Evangelist Kuhlman's life. Little did he know that coming into contact with her – and being under her tutelage – would have such a dramatic and powerful influence on his life and, ultimately, the lives of countless others through him.

Evangelist Hinn possesses the same kind of miracle and healing anointings as did Evangelist Kuhlman because he caught her mantle. Although they weren't her anointings to give, God ordained it to be so and endowed Evangelist Hinn with the same anointings. You see, miracles and healings needed to be continued. Anointings don't die with people since they come from God; they're passed on to those suited for them.

I don't doubt that others wear Evangelist Kuhlman's mantle anointings, especially those who were in her immediate sphere of influence. A biography of Evangelist Kathryn Kuhlman can be found in Roberts Liardon's book entitled, *God's Generals*.

Another example of a mantle anointing relationship – male to male – is Pastor Kenneth Copeland and Pastor Creflo Dollar. A definite mantle anointing relationship exists between the two. In fact, anyone who observes them carefully can clearly see the connection and hear the similarity in their speech.

One morning in June 2001, while getting ready for work, I had the television on so I could listen to it. I was confident that Pastor Kenneth Copeland was speaking, but – to my surprise – when I turned around and looked at the television, Pastor Creflo Dollar was speaking. Had I not looked to see who was speaking, you couldn't tell me otherwise. Clearly, a unique mantle anointing relationship exists between the two. They speak the same language, sound the same, and have a similar teaching style – so similar they even have the same mannerisms. Both their ministries tend to focus on the same areas, such as prosperity, faith, finances, and the like.

This next example of a modern-day mantle anointing relationship doesn't stop with one catcher.

The thrower has mentored many individuals who have gone on to become pastors, ministers, and leaders both locally and countrywide. I had the honor of interviewing this powerful mentor – Bishop Dr. Gwendolyn G. Weeks, affectionately known as Dr. Weeks – who pastors her own church in Boston, Massachusetts, leads the Eastern Cape Diocese of the Pentecostal Assemblies of the World (PAW) in South Africa, and is a missionary to several churches on the Continent of Africa.

During the interview, I asked Dr. Weeks the following questions:

Question #1: In your own words, how would you define a mantle anointing relationship?

Response: *"It has to be a relationship of intimacy, nakedness, and willingness [of the mentee] to be cut and to submit to the cutting. If I'm to be your father [spiritually], you have to allow me to circumcise you."* [Brackets added].

Let's not forget the importance of accountability on the part of the mentee, which ties into intimacy. One can't be accountable without his or her mentor being privy to his or her personal life as is appropriate.

Question #2: Do you believe that mentoring falls under the umbrella of mantle anointing relationships?

Response: *"It depends on what mentees want. There are those who have received it and are running with it and those who take it like a menu and pick and choose. There are those who will pick it* [the mantle] *up and wear it and those who won't."* [Brackets added].

In my own personal experience of being a mentor, most of the individuals I mentored in the past didn't truly want to be mentored. They wanted something else. Or once they realized what it involved, they decided it wasn't for them. Perhaps others competed for their time and attention, causing them to abandon the process. Still others may have treated them as their own personal 'property', not allowing anyone else to mentor or pour into them.

Question #3: Without naming anyone, can you share an example of when you mentored someone, and it evolved into a mantle anointing relationship? What was the process? What was the outcome for the mentee?

Response: *"My process is taking people through discipleship. I have monthly meetings with my mentees. There is intimacy. It's not just meeting at the church. We dine together, play games, visit each other's homes. Even when spending time with my young people, I always have questions ready to ask them. I make myself available to them."*

True mentors are proactive. They're not sitting back waiting on their mentee to ask them questions or to say what the need is. Truthfully, sometimes mentees don't know what to ask. Mentors must be equipped to ask the right questions – to probe with caution and boundaries in place. That's what the relationship is all about.

Question #4: You caught the mantle of your late father. What was the process like? When did you know you were being groomed to be his successor?

Response: *"What I do comes from my father – both of my parents. I didn't have my own vision. I am continuing the vision of my father. My parents would travel to Montserrat every year with barrels of goods for those in need.*

As a missionary, I travel to Africa with goods to bless those in need. The same is true of the food pantry at my local church. It's to bless those locally who are in need.

My father raised me and my siblings to do what he did – to be a worker in the church locally and to serve abroad as a missionary. This started from my childhood. I did everything in the church.

I was already an evangelist and had gone to seminary. When my father decided to step down [throw his mantle], *I came back home to become pastor* [catcher] *– to be his successor. I was ready. I had been trained all of my life. I was installed as pastor in December 1994."* [Brackets added].

Dr. Weeks' response to this last question made me think upon Jesus. During His earthly ministry, He did what His father told Him to do. He didn't have His own agenda (John 6:38-40, 5:17) He proclaimed, *"I and my Father are one"* (John 10:30, KJV). As we work for the Lord, we must not forget those in our Jerusalem. It's easy to go beyond those in our immediate sphere of influence to help others while those in our Jerusalem go lacking.

The final thought that Dr. Weeks shared with me is that she doesn't mentor people out of state or locally from other churches. The reason is because – first and foremost – they need to be mentored by their own pastor. She only mentors those in her own house or church. She needs to be able to see her mentees, develop intimacy, chastise them, instruct them, and do all the things that come with mentoring. She stated, *"It takes time to be with someone."*

I want to thank Dr. Weeks for her willingness to be interviewed and to share candidly. Her ministry has touched my life and is impactful, far-reaching, and as authentic as they come.

May God bless her and her church family – the great house of Bethel Tabernacle Pentecostal Church.

Chapter 10: The Relational Aspect of Reconciliation & the Fruit of the Spirit

As human beings, maintaining the right relationships can sometimes be challenging. Every now and then we may experience a bad relationship – some more than others. Let us explore a few things that might help us as we are exposed to difficulties with others – and them with us – for the sake of being in mantle anointing relationships and right relationships. Moreover, consider this question as food for thought: Does God pair up only those He knows will get along or like each other?

Reconciliation

Reconciliation is one of the terms used in describing salvation because the act of reconciliation has to do with renewing friendships and relationships that have been severed or damaged. Reconciliation is an adjustment process that works through trespasses made against another person, allowing individuals to become friendly or harmonious again. Reconciliation brings submission back into our lives like what Christ did for us. He adjusted our relationship with God the Father, bringing harmony and thereby giving us the ability to submit so that God's purpose could be carried out in our lives. This work afforded us the opportunity to enjoy the benefits God gave us through Jesus Christ (Ephesians 2:4-10). Not only has Jesus Christ brought reconciliation to us, He has given us the word of reconciliation according to II Corinthians 5:19-21.

Looking at reconciliation from a salvation perspective, it delivers the message to humanity that their sins are no longer being held against them and that they can receive forgiveness of sins through Jesus Christ.

This is the message God has given us as we are the best ones to deliver it to others since we have experienced the reconciling favor of God in our lives. Reconciliation is critical to healthy relationships – so much that Jesus said, *"So, if you are standing before the altar in the Temple, offering a sacrifice to God, and you suddenly remember that someone has something against you, leave your sacrifice there beside the altar. Go and be reconciled to that person. Then come and offer your sacrifice to God* (Matthew 5:23-24, NLT).

The Bible lets us know that being out of harmony with each other affects our sacrifice or worship to God. Needless to say, those who are destined to be in mantle anointing relationships must be able to work through their differences, recognizing that God has put them together for greater purposes than their own.

Reconciliation calls for one or both persons to submit to each other. To submit, one of the parties must choose to be the listener. There are times when one of the parties will have to be willing to take the blame or relinquish his or her rights to be brought into harmony with the other person. We learn this discipline by first submitting to God through the work of the Holy Spirit in our hearts. Submitting to each other can be difficult if we have not first submitted to God. Ephesians 2 is a perfect example of how Jesus abolished the wall of hostility, showing us that His initial work was to reconcile groups set against each other. This work has been completed through the life, death, and resurrection of Jesus Christ. Furthermore, we are made alive with Christ, which enables us to submit to God and each other.

When reconciliation occurs, individuals come together – the total opposite of what would happen without the work of reconciliation.

Reconciliation brings about a sincere, earnest commitment between those involved to work in harmony, putting aside differences that would hinder the progress of the work and the relationship.

Let us explore another avenue by which we can have right relationships. Examining what right relationships are made up of makes clear the fact that enemies don't have wholesome, healthy relationships. The word *'enemies'* imply that people are against each other, disliking each other. Healthy relationships exist when those involved have genuine and sincere intentions toward each other. Intention is the key. Right relationships are built on trust, honesty, loyalty, mutual respect, and support of one another. One thing – among many – that *can* kill right relationships is unchecked insecurity.

Let's face it! Sometimes it's easier to support others when we're involved in their project, are on the same level, or will personally gain something from supporting them. Easier, but not always right. Supporting an individual is easy when we're progressing at the same rate. On the contrary, there's a fine line between giving support and feeling insecure or even threatened by the one being supported. There are many contributors to one feeling insecure – childhood and life experiences, self-doubt and negative beliefs, etc. Insecurity can destroy right relationships.

Mantle anointing relationships can draw out one's insecurity. Insecurity has to do with a lack of confidence in one's own abilities or potential. When an individual feels threatened by the abilities of another, it can cause him or her to become insecure. Such a feeling of threat can kill the purpose of the relationship, making it difficult to progress with this obstacle in the way. One of the purposes of mantle anointing relationships is to build confidence, not break it. The relationship is to equip, train, support, and continue a work.

An individual's insecurity rising to the surface is not necessarily a bad thing *if* he or she is willing to put in the inward work needed to change his or her mindset to combat that insecurity.

Because we are accomplishing God's mission and not our own, we should make every effort to move beyond our superficial insecurities and focus on the mission.

The opposite of insecurity is confidence. Confidence is strengthened as one begins to exercise his or her abilities regularly – whether as a thrower or catcher. Insecurities should not be allowed to take root or fester no more than individuals should allow themselves to become threatened by another's abilities.
It's best to address and work towards resolving insecurities early in the relationship as they can lead to conflict and ultimately end the relationship.

Most commonly, insecurities tend to appear in the catchers – mentees – but that doesn't mean throwers – mentors – don't experience insecurity. After all, they are grooming others to do the same or similar work as themselves, and – in some cases – to become their successor. Because the emphasis of such relationships is ultimately to continue a work already begun, throwers should do all they can to boost confidence in catchers, especially since throwers are seen as being more experienced and mature.

An open line of communication is one of the things that helps to strengthen confidence. If catchers feel they can ask the thrower anything pertaining to the specialized training or task, their confidence is more likely to be built up. Furthermore, availability helps to boost confidence. The availability of throwers is salient in giving catchers access to them as much as possible.

Likewise, catchers need to make themselves available and ready to do their part in the relationship, even if it's just to observe and serve.

Operating insecurely is operating in the flesh. The Apostle Paul admonishes us not to be ruled by our flesh, but by the Spirit (Galatians 5:25). The Kingdom of God is spiritual. To accomplish and fulfill kingdom work, we must operate in the Spirit, not the flesh. Naturally, a kingdom is an undivided territory that is subject to a king or monarch. Within the kingdom, there are citizens that obey the rules governing that kingdom. The subject of kingdom building and the kingdom itself will be discussed further later.

Fruit of the Spirit

But when the Holy Spirit controls our lives, he will produce this kind of fruit in us: love, joy, peace, patience, kindness, goodness, faithfulness, gentleness, and self-control. Here there is no conflict with the law.

Those who belong to Christ Jesus have nailed the passions and desires of their sinful nature to his cross and crucified them there. If we are living now by the Holy Spirit, let us follow the Holy Spirit's leading in every part of our lives. Let us not become conceited, or irritate one another, or be jealous of one another (Galatians 5:22-26, NLT). Ephesians 5:9-10 says, *"For this light within you produces only what is good and right and true. Try to find out what is pleasing to the Lord."* (NLT).

The fruit of the Spirit is necessary in right relationships. If we were led by our own feelings or mood, there are times that we would not make an effort to be in right relationships.

The fact that the fruit – embodying various characteristics or character traits – originates from God and not from our carnal nature reassures us that we can have healthy, lasting, and productive relationships.

The keyword in Galatians 5:22 is *'control.'* It takes ongoing effort to live a life that is controlled by the Holy Spirit. Clearly, the only way we can be guided is if we submit. Submission opens the door for someone else to lead the way.
Furthermore, yielding grants permission for another person to lead. When we yield to the Holy Spirit, we allow Him to produce in our lives what is pleasing to Him.

In Ephesians 5:9, Paul tells us that the Light – Holy Spirit – which dwells in us only produces what is good, right, and true. Obviously, before we can see such production in ourselves, we must yield to God. Yielding to God causes us to be conformed to the image of His Son Jesus Christ – the One who reconciled us to God the Father (Romans 8:29). Without first submitting to God, submitting to one another can be difficult. Moreover, it's good to be aware that just because two people work together doesn't mean they will get along or agree on every aspect of work and how to do it.

The exploration of reconciliation – through the fruit of the Spirit – shows us how it can greatly assist us in learning to submit to one another and thereby cooperate for the purpose of mantle anointing relationships and right relationships.

Chapter 11: Covenant Relationships

Mantle anointing relationships can be looked upon as covenant relationships between those that honor, trust, and respect each other. Those who do not have these traits at work in themselves cannot enter covenant relationships without them being present. A covenant is unique because it is a binding mutual agreement of sorts between two people. Emphasis is placed on the word *binding*. Under such conditions, the agreement can only be carried out between the two, linking them together for a certain period of time. It's a partnership of sorts between individuals who have something in common naturally or spiritually.

Typically, covenants are not meant to be broken, but it happens. There are two kinds of covenants: conditional and unconditional. Conditional covenants are based on the recipient doing what is required to obtain the promise of the covenant from the covenant maker. Unconditional covenants don't need anything on the part of the recipient. The fulfillment of the promise depends solely on the covenant maker.

Conditional Covenant = Requires response [action] on the part of the recipient. The proper response = Outcome [fulfillment of the promise] on the part of the covenant maker.

Unconditional Covenant = Fulfillment [manifestation] of the promise depends on the covenant maker. The recipient of the covenant does not have to do anything to secure and obtain the promise but to remain in a state of readiness.

David and Jonathan had a covenant relationship.
As for you, show kindness to your servant, for you have brought him into a covenant with you before the LORD. (I Samuel 20:8, NIV).

While Saul was trying to kill David, he (David) covenanted with Jonathan for his own safety and protection. Jonathan promised to see to it that David received whatever he desired. David trusted Jonathan enough to give him specific instructions of what he should say *if* Saul inquired about him.

The covenant between David and Jonathan could not be executed without mutual love and respect between the two (I Samuel 20:1-13, 41-42).

God ordains covenant relationships. Thus, this kind of relationship should not be compared to or considered to be a contractual type of agreement. It is different. Contracts are based on distrust, which is the reason why signatures are required. Once an individual puts his signature on a contract, he or she has sealed the agreement. By the same token, if he or she puts his or her signature on a contractual agreement but does not follow through with the conditions and timeline of the deal, then he or she becomes susceptible to the actions, repercussions, or consequences of breaking the contract. Contractual agreements are natural and are sealed on earth – in the earthly realm. On the contrary, covenant agreements are spiritual and are sealed in heaven.

Covenant agreements don't require signatures since they are based on trust and respect. Therefore, one who puts trust in another does not look for proof to validate *that* trust. God places trust in us, although He has every reason not to. Believing that God trusts and respects us is difficult to receive, yet He does. Throughout generations, it is evident that God establishes and enters this unique relationship with His people. From Genesis to Revelation, God initiated some type of covenant relationship with specific people, groups, or races of people, and, in some cases, He established covenant agreements that would – in some way – affect the entire human race.

When it comes to God, we don't need to concern ourselves with whether He will break a covenant. A covenant between God and humans can be damaged if it's a conditional covenant, and the requirements are not upheld by humans. In this case, the covenant is ended.

Knowing that we don't make covenant agreements with God and that He makes them with us is principal. We can't initiate covenants with God because we don't have what it takes in our humanity to approach God on that level. God draws us into specific covenant relationships based on our individual relationship with Him and the call He places on our lives.

Covenant relationships are more than ordinary relationships. They are special and unique. A close bond and fellowship exist in covenant relationships. Those involved in this relationship recognize the significance of it, including events and places linking them together.

Mantle anointing relationships consist of covenant agreements – to some degree – between those involved. Often, those covenant agreements are unspoken, meaning there's a bond that connects the two, bearing witness that it's more than an ordinary relationship – like pregnant Mary and Elizabeth (Luke 1:39-42). Moving forward in mantle anointing relationships without knowing what's expected or working together towards a common goal can be arduous.

Promotion and progression in this relationship are dependent on how well individuals connect as covenant partners. It's impossible to be in a mantle anointing relationship and not be in covenant with each other – on the work that is taking place.
A covenant is an agreement, but don't get hung up on the formality of it because – as I said earlier – the agreement can be present without being documented or even spoken of – initially.

The agreement takes place on the inside of both individuals. It's a spiritual agreement. As individuals spend time together, focusing on the work, it will be clear what the covenant agreement is.
At that point, both persons should agree upon what the relationship is, embodies, and will produce.

As stated earlier, covenants are spiritual. In mantle anointing relationships, covenants are perceived – envisioned and understood – in the spirit realm. There's always a spiritual aspect to understanding the relationship. Knowing this about covenant relationships is vital since things won't always be clearly understood in the natural realm. In other words, that which is expected to transpire in covenant relationships may not make sense in the natural realm – to the natural mind – at first.

Therefore, one's spiritual state of mind is a crucial factor at this level of relationship, which is where the trust factor comes in – not just trusting God but trusting each other. Trust ensures dependence. Both parties depend on God, but they also depend on each other to follow through and maintain a certain level of spirituality, integrity, and character so that the covenant – which was established in heaven – can be manifested on earth. Dependence means more than just looking to the other person to do his or her part. It also means recognizing that the individual is equipped and capable of performing.

Furthermore, confidentiality is an essential component of covenant relationships. The ability to keep the confidences of those directly involved affects the growth and progression of the relationship. There are times when the covenant agreement set forth in mantle anointing relationships is meant only for those directly involved to hear, know, and discuss. What destroys trust in such relationships is breaking confidence where it is needed and expected. Such an act of betrayal can also be described as a breach of confidence.

Breach of confidence – as it pertains to covenant agreements – means that an individual has disclosed or shared the contents of the covenant to an outsider or one that is outside of that particular relationship without permission.

When God gives us a glimpse of something, we're sometimes eager to share what He has shown us publicly. To this end, there are times when we need to keep – hide in order to preserve – what God has shown us until He releases us to share if He releases us. Similarly, the rule applies to mantle anointing covenant relationships. Avoiding sharing prematurely that which we ourselves don't fully understand is pivotal.

People have things in their lives that they feel emotionally connected to or sentimental about. For some, it's not that those things are needed any longer but that they remind them of a particular event, person, or season in their lives. There's sentimental value. Long after covenant agreements have been fulfilled and catchers become successors and throwers are promoted to other tasks, there remains some sort of connection and remembrance of the relationship that existed between the two.

Chapter 12: The Fitting for a Mantle Anointing Relationship ~ The Dressmaker

Being fitted for a mantle anointing is a selection and preparation process. When Elijah threw his mantle on Elisha in I Kings 19:19, it was a natural act with a spiritual implication. I believe that act conveyed – in part – that both individuals knew their spiritual *identity*.

Identity is vital in mantle anointing relationships; it is comprised of more than a person's physical presence. Identity encompasses all that a person is made up of, such as one's beliefs and values, natural abilities, spiritual gifts, cultural background and upbringing. Identity introduces two main aspects; first, who we are perceived to be naturally speaking and second, who we are from a spiritual standpoint. Of course, the latter has greater significance.

Lack of knowing one's identity in Christ blurs any task, causing an individual to lack direction, confidence, and, ultimately, an understanding of his or her God-ordained purpose. On the contrary, an individual who is confident about his or her identity has an advantage in carrying out God's will because he or she doesn't have to deal with the issue of insecurity. Identity can be strengthened – more clearly defined – in mantle anointing relationships.

In scripture, mentees were usually selected to wear their mentor's mantle upon the near completion of a particular work as performed by their mentor. We can refer to this act as a changing of the guards. Throughout scripture, God strategically connected people to work together, knowing that the players would change at the appointed time. This selection process can be looked at as the actual fitting stage of the relationship.

In the spirit realm, the passing of a mantle signifies a fitting between two equals, almost like shopping for items that come in pairs. For example, an individual may enter a store, see shoes he or she likes, but notice there's only one shoe on the rack or in the window. Since he or she really likes the style of that particular shoe, he or she will search the store or ask the store clerk for assistance in locating the other shoe. Once that other shoe is found and is put with the other one, they make a pair that's wearable. If the other pair cannot be found, the one shoe is no good to anyone. A mantle anointing fitting works just like that; it is a fitting or 'pairing up of equals' to accomplish a mission or work. As God selects individuals to 'wear' an anointing for the purpose of executing a task, this fitting takes place. However, the wearer – mentee – may not know in advance that he or she is being considered to wear a mantle anointing whereas the thrower – mentor – may receive instructions from God as to who should receive his or her mantle.

In a fitting for a mantle anointing, development is vital in order to ensure a proper fitting. The development stage can be likened to the role of a dressmaker in relation to his or her customer. When someone goes to a dressmaker to be fitted for a garment, several things must happen. The person for which the garment is being made needs to have an initial meeting with the dressmaker to communicate his or her wishes. During the initial meeting – if the customer has not already decided on the pattern, type of fabric and texture, and other specifics – he or she will be asked questions about these things. Additionally, the dressmaker may ask about the occasion for which the garment is being made.

Knowing the occasion gives the dressmaker a better understanding of what the customer wants and helps him or her to make recommendations for the benefit of the customer.

Most importantly, measurements of the customer are taken so that the dressmaker knows the amount of fabric to use to accommodate the customer's needs. If the dressmaker is tasked with providing the fabric, he or she should provide more than what's needed. That way, there'll be more than enough fabric to accommodate changes along the way. All these steps are taken so the customer's needs could be met in a satisfactory manner.

The customer would then visit the dressmaker a second time to try on the garment in an unfinished state – a state in which the garment has been based and not sewn as a final product. During this 'trying on' stage, clothing being worn by the customer must first be removed in order to try on what has been made, to get the most accurate fit. Furthermore, putting on clothing on top of other clothing is not recommended in this case as it prevents a proper fitting and hinders the individual from seeing and appreciating the full beauty of what is being tried on.

When God calls us into mantle anointing relationships, He expects us to rid ourselves of things in our lives that may be a hindrance to such relationships; He will let us know what those things are although most times we are very much aware of what they are. Moreover, there are times when God expects us to unlearn what we feel we know so well that we may gain new perspectives on how He wants to work in and through us.

As the customer tries on the new garment, a few things *may* occur. Although the customer was pre-measured for the garment, once it is sewn or made it may be too small or, for some reason, too big. Inaccurate sizing could mean that the dressmaker's initial measurements were off or that he or she isn't very skilled in that area. It could also mean the customer's weight has changed. The dressmaker would have no need to panic *if* he or she has more than enough fabric and providing the pattern's simple enough to alter.

Dealing with a professional, experienced dressmaker increases the chances of getting a garment that's a perfect fit the first time around, needing only finishing touches to complete the job.

When relying on human judgment, there's always the possibility of errors. In the event that the garment is too big, it could simply be a matter of re-measuring the individual and cutting the fabric down to size. Once again, it all depends on the complexity of the pattern and the expertise of the dressmaker. When the customer has been fitted once or twice, the dressmaker then works toward completing the job. Completion includes adding all the finishing touches such as buttons and/or zippers, special cuffs, and the like. These things are crucial to the overall appearance of the garment and take precision, careful concentration, and steady hands.

Sometimes the smaller, less apparent things take more time and patience and require more work. Nonetheless, once those things are done correctly – the finishing touches – they're usually the first things others notice and admire when the garment is worn. People appreciate the effort that goes into the fine details of a task or project, enhancing the overall appearance or function.
God works in us this way: He works on all the fine details that others can't see – from the inside out –to make us better.

The illustration of the dressmaker, in relationship to the customer, gives us a better understanding of the important stage of development in being fitted for a mantle anointing. The difference between being fitted naturally versus spiritually is that spiritually, God does the fitting. He is the Dressmaker. God knows our size, shape, and height, perfectly eliminating possibilities for making errors when it comes to an actual fitting. Errors occur when *we* deter from God's instructions. God also knows our weight capacity in terms of what we can 'house,' hold, or contain.

He knows the depth of our being and selects the type of garment – anointing – that is most fitting for us. While dressmakers are servants completely in that they cater to the needs of the customer, God is our Heavenly Father, shaping us according to His plans and purposes, not our wants.

We all would like to have certain things in life in our possession. We see things that we like, yet the attraction doesn't mean we should have those things or that they are right for us. For example, when someone goes shopping for clothing, he or she may see items of interest, but that doesn't mean just any item will look good on him or her. Many have had the experience of entering clothing stores that carry styles they like; however, when they tried on the clothes, they soon realized that not everything looks good on them. Truthfully, some articles of clothing look better on a hanger. Not all styles, colors, and shapes look good on everyone. That's a fact! Spiritually, when it comes to the gifts of the Spirit and the anointing, God gives us the gift and anointing-style that are suitable for our calling and character. For example, some may have the gift of healing but, instead, desire the gift to teach. God knows which gift is better for each person because He knows what we're made of.

When God does the fitting, He makes no mistakes. God is perfect and holy, and His measurements are precise! We, on the other hand, don't always appreciate the fitting, perhaps because we can't see the big picture of what God wants to do in our lives. For this reason, things can quickly get messed up with our human involvement. God wants us to be perfect and holy. But first, we must have the proper perception of what perfection is.

We view perfection much differently than God does. We tend to think that perfection means an individual is flawless and makes no mistakes. However, scripture teaches us that perfection has to do with reaching a level of spiritual maturity.

With maturity comes development – naturally and spiritually – knowledge, wisdom in life and decision-making, thoughtfulness, and insight. All of these qualities help us to weigh situations, acknowledging the advantages and disadvantages, before proceeding.

Being fitted for a mantle anointing requires the fine details of timing and discernment, which are equally as important as those things that enhance the performance of and bring clarity to the role of a dressmaker. Additionally, the fine details in mantle anointing relationships include ongoing fellowship between the mentor and mentee – fellowship in prayer being united with the same mind as it pertains to their roles and assignments. Knowing our part in such relationships helps us to avoid getting involved in areas that we're not called to or prepared for. Not everyone is equipped to be a leader, neither is everyone equipped to be an administrator, but everyone is equipped to fill *some* role.

The Development Stage

During the development stage, adequate training becomes a key component to the success of those involved in mantle anointing relationships. Development goes hand-in-hand with training and preparation.

Notwithstanding, development focuses more specifically on areas that an individual will be utilized in rather than general areas. Such concentration allows an individual to see what he or she is really good at. Thus, development has to do with testing one's abilities. During the testing process, how well or effectively a person can perform a particular task is measured. The purpose of testing is to verify deliverables – to ensure that needs are met. If anything will expose defects, imperfections, unpreparedness, and inadequacies, it's testing! Tests reveals how much people know; thereby, disclosing what they don't know.

Furthermore, tests determine how well an individual can perform, function, or thrive in environments that are conducive for success, challenges, and adversity. Testing, then, measures a person's efficiency-level, dependability, effectiveness, flexibility, and elasticity – stretch-ability – showing both surpluses and deficits.

Based on the results of a test, an individual will then know the areas he or she needs to spend more time developing. The maturation of development depends – in part – on one's strengths and weaknesses and how prepared he or she is in seeing and seizing opportunities that exist. With some opportunities, there are also threats. How individuals handle threats – challenges – will either enhance or hinder their development stage. In the business world, such a concept is referred to as a SWOT analysis – <u>S</u>trengths, <u>W</u>eaknesses, <u>O</u>pportunities, and <u>T</u>hreats. This framework is accredited to Albert Humphrey, who developed the approach back in the 1960s and early 1970s. We must recognize and address each of these areas in our own lives by looking at the data – the track record, the proof, the facts. We must know these things about ourselves and work towards developing those areas in which we are weak or lack.

When opportunities come, we should examine what threats may exist, if any, especially when making or considering life-altering decisions. However, just because there are 'threats' doesn't mean we can't be successful in the opportunities God gives us. After all, we have His grace – His empowerment and strength. We simply need to develop an effective plan – with God's leading and help – that will combat potential threats. Such a plan includes prayer. As the children of Israel prepared for entry into the land of Canaan, Moses sent out twelve spies to survey the land. But of the twelve, only two spies (Joshua and Caleb) returned with positive reports that Israel could take the land.

The survey was necessary because Moses needed to know what potential threats he faced bringing the children of Israel into the Promised Land – such as who occupied the land, how many of them there were, and the physical size and strength of the people.

Walking by faith and trusting in God's power, as we must, are not licenses for ignorance about our surroundings. Additionally, laziness and fear are also factors preventing us from fulfilling our God-ordained purpose. Once we become aware that a problem exists that could hamper or hinder our progress, we lean on the Lord, inviting His wisdom and instruction on what to do about it. That's a plan that will work!

During the development stage, many things rise to the surface and many discoveries are made. At times, we don't notice our own abilities or realize they exist until we are put in a position where they are needed. It is then that those abilities become paramount in our mind. There are hidden treasures within us. These hidden treasures can be described in one word – potential. We may not recognize our potential at first, and it may not be fully developed; nonetheless, potential exists. God knows what's in us; we just need to depend on Him to help us bring those things out.

In the development stage, the value of preparation is vital. At some point, there must be a scaling down of responsibilities or areas focused on, leading to those things that are specifically geared towards the area one will function in – ultimately. One of the reasons *some* students study double majors is because they are uncertain – or undecided – about the area they would like to concentrate on. Preparation certainly involves a wide range of skill-development, activities, and learning aids. We should spend more time developing specialized skills that are needed for the task at hand.

Self-development requires knowing yourself. There are individuals who don't see the value in taking time to really know themselves. There are those who reject themselves. Self-rejection turns into self-defeat, working against the self-development process. Furthermore, failure to set realistic goals – among other things – works against self-development. Goals must be within one's reach. Goals can't be vague; they must be clear. Specificity is crucial in setting goals. Goals must have a start date and an end date. Stretching goals well beyond the end date could be an indication that an area went lacking or something went wrong with the process itself.

If adequate development is not sought out and invested in, then a perfect fitting in a mantle anointing relationship becomes challenging, if not impossible. An individual needs to ensure his or her own self-development even when in a mantle anointing relationship. Personal development – with applied discipline – among other things ensures that an expands upon the right skill set for a particular task, to successfully accomplish it. To assist with proper development, it's important to measure the desired – but realistic – end result by the tasks to be accomplished, and not necessarily by the personal preferences of those involved in the tasks.

Proper development ensures a clearer view of what needs to occur. If one can see his or her way clearly, then it becomes easier to reach his or her destination with focus and without giving way to distractions.

Chapter 13: Catching the Mantle ~ From Preparation to Possession

A mantle anointing is passed down from thrower to catcher, not up or horizontally. Luke 6:40 says, *"A disciple is not above his teacher, but everyone who is perfectly trained will be like his teacher"* (NKJV). The same rule applies between the thrower and catcher. The catcher may not start out on the same level as the thrower in certain areas, but by the time he or she becomes a successor, he or she will be *like* the mentor.

Catching the mantle speaks of a readiness to possess a specialized anointing on the part of the catcher and the readiness to be discharged from a task or role on the part of the thrower. This position of readiness shows that the catcher has passed through all the stages of the preparation process and is ready to possess the mantle.

Possession, then, speaks of ownership and ownership suggests that one knows his or her rights and privileges, embraces them, and isn't afraid to exercise authority within those rights. Confidence of ownership dismisses insecurity. Thus, an individual doesn't wonder whether a particular thing is within his or her possession; no, one knows it! There's a secure confidence in the heart of the one who possesses.

As God positions individuals to catch the mantle of throwers, He qualifies and equips them for special tasks and they, in turn, have the responsibility of walking more boldly in that anointing. The Holy Spirit gives boldness to His people.

Catching the mantle is the final endorsement of a mentee's readiness to move forward as a successor.

Nevertheless, if an individual isn't watchful to see – spiritually and symbolically – the mantle when it falls from his or her predecessor, then he or she won't obtain a double portion anointing.

Elijah's mantle fell to the ground, but Elisha did not leave it there; he picked it up. Be ready to step into your role or position by picking up the mantle!

"He [Elisha] took up also the mantle of Elijah that fell from him, and went back and stood by the bank of Jordan; (II Kings 2:13, KJV)".

The greater responsibility of catching the mantle is placed upon the recipient thereof – the mentee – and not the thrower – mentor. Once throwers cast their mantle, their job ends in a particular area of responsibility or specific physical or geographical location. Mentees must position themselves in ways that ensure they will not miss their opportunity to become successors by paying careful attention to their thrower. To do so, mentees must carefully observe the progression of their predecessor and listen – not just hear – what the predecessor is communicating to them, so they will know when that individual is ready to completely turn a specific work over into their care.

In the transference stage of the relationship, paying careful attention to the words, actions, and behavior of the thrower is especially salient for the catcher. If the two people are well connected prior to this stage, the right time to make the transition will be evident to both. If they are not well connected, it may not be as obvious or communicated clearly as to when the exact 'finishing time' of the thrower will be. To avoid a disconnection, catchers need to be ready at all times. Be ready.

At this point, reiterating the fact that Elisha picked up Elijah's mantle is worthwhile. Elisha had the spiritual sense to pick up the mantle. He pressed in. Elijah didn't tell him to pick up the mantle. He said, if you see me when I am taken away from you, then you will have what you asked for. Surely, Elisha saw, and then he acted. He moved. This point must be remembered (II Kings 2:13-14). Prior to this instance, the only other recorded time that Elisha came into contact with Elijah's mantle was when Elijah first threw his mantle on him in I Kings 19:19. Elisha knew what his purpose was, and he knew that it connected him to the life of Elijah. Therefore, picking up Elijah's mantle from the ground was symbolically important to Elisha.

Let's dig deeper. Elijah had already told Elisha that he had asked for a difficult thing in requesting an *inheritance* of a double portion of his (Elijah's) anointing (II Kings 2:9-12). This is power-packed! Elisha's request was difficult but not impossible. In I Kings 19:19, Elijah's mantle over Elisha's shoulders was an act of adoption. He adopted him as a son. From that very moment, Elijah invested in him the prophetic office. This wasn't something Elijah did haphazardly; no, he knew what he was doing. He saw fruit in Elisha's life. Fruit can't grow without seed – planted in good ground, watered, nourished, and receiving light from the Son. Jesus Christ adopted us as sons – no gender attached – when we weren't son material. The word *'son'* is a Greek word. We are adopted because our Thrower – Jesus Christ – gave His life for us to redeem us from the hand of the enemy and to reconcile us to the Father. (See Ephesians 1:3-8, 2:19-22; Galatians 4:5-7, 3:26; I John 3:1-3, 10; John 1:12;Romans 8:14-23; Matthew 5:45; John 3:16). Sons have access. Biblically, an inheritance is left to sons.

Sons can ask for what they want as long as it's in the will of God, but they shouldn't ask aimlessly or unknowingly (Matthew 7:7-8).

You may be asking, "What else was significant about Elisha picking up the mantle? Why not leave it on the ground? I want to ask you, "Would the Jordan River have parted for Elisha if he did not use Elijah's mantle to strike the water?" Let's look at II Kings 2:10 again. Elijah said to Elisha, *"If you see me when I am taken from you, then you will get your request."* Elijah said nothing about Elisha having to pick up his mantle.

During the transitional stage, from preparation to possession, the mentee receives the covering of the mentor. The significance of Elijah throwing his mantle on Elisha in I Kings 19:19 is very different than when Elisha picked up Elijah's mantle in II Kings 2:13. The act performed in I Kings 19:19 was done as the initial stage of Elisha's call, training, and preparation for his succession role. On the contrary, what transpired in II Kings 2:13 – Elijah being taken away and Elisha picking up his mantle – served as a symbol of Elisha's authority as a prophet. Elisha literally stepped into the authority of Elijah. With this authority, Elisha used Elijah's mantle to part the Jordan River as Elijah had previously done (II Kings 2:13-14).

Elisha may have also used the mantle as a way of fleecing God to confirm his appointment as Elijah's successor – if the water parted when he struck it with Elijah's mantle, it meant the anointing of Elijah was upon him. If the water didn't part, it meant he was not anointed in Elijah's place. We know this is true because Elisha asked the question after he struck the water, *"Where is the Lord God of Elijah?"* Elisha wanted to know that God was with him as He had been with Elijah. Sure enough, the water parted, and Elisha went across to the other side. This occurrence was a visible endorsement that Elisha had been anointed as Elijah's successor.

Elisha picked up Elijah's mantle off the ground as a form of covering himself. Elijah's mantle had symbolic value to Elisha.

Although Elisha – by virtue of the fact that he saw Elijah being taken away – received a double portion of Elijah's anointing, the mantle was all that was left of Elijah that he could identify with. The double portion that Elisha received was an inheritance of a lifetime of work, preparation, sacrifice, tests, hiding in fear, and victories that Elijah experienced. Therefore, inheritances should not be squandered. They are valuable. More than receiving an inheritance of works, Elisha received an inheritance of qualities from Elijah.

We looked at how Elisha caught the mantle of Elijah under the Old Testament, taking him from preparation to possession. Let's look at how those in the upper room in Jerusalem – in the book of Acts – caught the mantle of Jesus Christ.

During the forty days after His [Jesus'] crucifixion, He appeared to the apostles from time to time and proved to them in many ways that He was actually alive. On those occasions, He talked to them about the Kingdom of God. In one of those meetings, Jesus shared a meal with them and instructed them, saying, *"Do not leave Jerusalem until the Father sends you what he promised. Remember, I have told you about this before. John baptized with water, but in just a few days you will be baptized with the Holy Spirit. On the day of Pentecost, seven weeks after Jesus' resurrection, the believers were meeting together in one place. Suddenly, there was a sound from heaven like the roaring of a mighty windstorm in the skies above them, and it filled the house where they were meeting. Then, what looked like flames or tongues of fire appeared and settled on each of them. And everyone present was filled with the Holy Spirit and began speaking in other languages, as the Holy Spirit gave them this ability"* (Acts 1:3-5, 2:1-4, NLT; brackets added).

Being in the right place was necessary for receiving the promise of the Holy Spirit on the day of Pentecost.

What was needed for those in the upper room to catch the mantle differed from what Elisha had to do to catch Elijah's mantle. Elisha was instructed to *watch*. Those in the upper room were instructed to *wait* in Jerusalem for the promise of the Holy Spirit. In Elisha's case, his eyes had to be fastened on Elijah since that would determine whether he would receive a double portion anointing. Those in the upper room had to wait in a specific location – in anticipation – until the promise of the Holy Spirit was given. The Lord could have given them the Holy Spirit in any location, but what better place for an outpouring of the Holy Spirit than in Jerusalem where the Feast of Pentecost was being held.

This allowed for countless witnesses to hear, in their own languages, about the beautiful things God had done. Some may have rejected Christ previously, but that demonstration was undeniable, drawing thousands to Christ! Additionally, I believe the apostles' obedience counted on that day. Their waiting was not inactive; it was active. They did something while they waited – praised God. Had they gone against the Lord's instruction and waited in another city they would not have received the promise because they would have been in disobedience. Jesus told them where to wait. The point is not that geographical location matters to an omnipresent, omnipotent God, but that it matters to us – to what we receive. We must honor the Lord's timing and instructions.

In both cases, the catchers' – Elisha and those in the upper room – hearts and minds had to be fixed on receiving the special endowment and inheritance. The point is: the pre-requisite for catching a thrower's mantle may differ from person to person, so it's crucial that each individual listens for God to speak and follow His instructions carefully. The catcher's ability to follow instructions determines how timely and successfully he or she progresses in a mantle anointing relationship.

The instructions given to Elisha and those in the upper room may seem minute, but their ability to follow those instructions determined whether they would be endowed with the mantle anointing promised them.

Chapter 14: The Mantle Anointing of the Believer

As born-again believers, we have the mantle anointing of Jesus Christ in the person of the Holy Spirit. We have this anointing by virtue of the fact that the Holy Spirit lives within us. Second Corinthians 1:21-22 reads as follows, *"It is God who gives us, along with you, the ability to stand firm for Christ. He has commissioned us, and he has identified us as his own by placing the Holy Spirit in our hearts as the first installment of everything he will give us"* (NLT). The mantle anointing of the Holy Spirit is an installment, indicating there is more! More power, greater ability, and more resources. Praise God!

Before Jesus Christ left the earth, He promised to send the Holy Spirit to all believers. *"And I will ask the Father, and he will give you another Advocate, who will never leave you. He is the Holy Spirit, who leads into all truth.* **The world cannot receive him, because it isn't looking for him and doesn't recognize him.** *But you know him, because he lives with you now and later will be in you. No, I will not abandon you as orphans – I will come to you"* (John 14:16-18, NLT).

Jesus kept His word in sending the Holy Spirit. John lets us know, in the book bearing his name, that the Holy Spirit is available to all those who believe in Jesus Christ (John 14:12). The Holy Spirit empowers us, giving us the ability to do far more (in our reach and through outlets) than Jesus was able to do during His earthly ministry. Today, advancing the Kingdom of God worldwide is much more achievable using the abundance of resources we have available to spread the gospel of Jesus Christ.

Let's look more closely at John 14:17. Jesus said, *"He is the Holy Spirit, who leads into all truth.*

The world cannot receive him, because it isn't looking for him and doesn't recognize him" (NLT). This verse falls in line with the one thing Elisha had to do – he had to *see* Elijah being taken away. Likewise, those who want the mantle anointing of Jesus Christ must prepare and position themselves for the gift of the Holy Spirit, look for Him – expect and anticipate His arrival – and receive Him. They must search the Bible on how to receive the Holy Spirit's mantle anointing – a promise – available to all believers.

Jesus said something significant in John 14:17 – *"...The world...cannot receive him...because it...doesn't recognize him."* That means the mantle anointing – Holy Spirit – is present in the world today. He's available to all who will receive Him, yet there are people who remain blinded by the god of this world. They can't even recognize that the Holy Spirit is hovering over the earth, waiting to endow His anointing upon those who want Him. What a tragedy!

Jesus knew His time on earth would be short, but we are an extension of Him. The same anointing that empowered Him to do what He did will perpetually empower us to continue *that* work if we let Him. We don't have 'new' work; we're continuing the work of the Lord. All Christian believers – upon their acceptance of the Lord Jesus Christ – have been pre-fitted for the mantle anointing of the Holy Spirit whether they realize it or operate in Him. This mantle anointing is what thrusts us forward, enabling us to fulfill God's purposes on earth.

As Christian believers, our understanding of the mantle anointing of the Holy Spirit should be that He's more than just an impartation. He is our helper. An impartation is receiving a part of a whole. If we compare the Old Testament prophets to those who receive the Holy Spirit today, the Spirit of God *rested* upon them at certain times for a particular work.

Today, we have the indwelling Holy Spirit. Often throughout the Old Testament we read the words, *"And the Spirit of the Lord was upon…"*. The Holy Spirit didn't reside within the Old Testament prophets as He was not yet given in that way. He rested upon them – a shadow of things to come.

The prophet Joel spoke of the coming outpouring of the Holy Spirit under the new covenant – New Testament – and that's what took place in the book of Acts (Joel 2:28-29; Acts 2). He now resides in us (John 15:16-21). Let's keep Him there and not grieve Him (Ephesians 4:30).

When the Holy Spirit was given to those in the upper room on the day of Pentecost, they received more than an impartation. They received baptism or full immersion *in* the Holy Spirit; He took up residence in their lives.

The mantle anointing Jesus left us is baptismal in nature, not with water but the same concept – full immersion *in* the grace, strength, supernatural ability, and authority of the Holy Spirit. We have been endowed!

It's a significant loss when we don't wear this anointing to the fullest extent. We make excuses about being human and, therefore, subject to failure. While that's true, we should ask ourselves, "When will I mature beyond this excuse and start becoming responsible and accountable with what God has given me? When will I begin to walk in the power of the Holy Spirit?"

If ever there's a time to wear the Holy Spirit's mantle anointing, it's now. The Lord didn't send Him to us for us to put Him on a shelf. We must allow Him to fill us, direct and lead us into all truth.

To wear His anointing means to rely on His power as we execute tasks, cooperating and functioning in agreement with Him.

To better understand the mantle anointing of the Holy Spirit, the Bible teaches that there are diversities of gifts but one Spirit who is the source of them all (I Corinthians 12:4). With diversities of gifts come diversities of anointings. There are different levels of anointing. For example, the person who operates in the gifts of healing is empowered specifically for *that* – healing. The person who operates in the word of wisdom is empowered for *that* specific gift. The anointing that rests upon us causes us to accomplish specialized and particular tasks, although the source of the anointing is the same – the Holy Spirit.

What occurred in Acts 2 resulted from Jesus Christ disrobing Himself, like removing a garment, and sending Himself back to those in the upper room and to as many as would receive Him. That wasn't only for then; it's for now. We must choose to wear [utilize] this anointing as an act of our will and as a new creation in Christ.

When Jesus sent the Holy Spirit, He sent all that we would ever need to continue God's work on earth and to sustain us. Being equipped in this manner is exactly why this mantle anointing is referred to as the 'greater works' anointing (John 14:12). In abundance we can continue the work that Christ began by drawing from the same source of power with the authority of God backing us. We have been equipped with a 'do more' mantle anointing.

Before the Holy Spirit was given, the apostles had the privilege and honor of being around Jesus day in and day out. We have the Word made flesh – the Logos – residing on the inside (John 1:14). If such an indwelling is not a mantle anointing, then I don't know what is.

The Lord Jesus Christ always impacted those around Him because He wore the mantle anointing of the Father. He was the Father incarnate. He was clear about His mission and declared it in Luke 4:18-19, which reads, *"The Spirit of the Lord is upon me, for he has anointed me to preach Good News to the poor. He has sent me to proclaim that captives will be released, that the blind will see, that the oppressed will be set free, and that the time of the Lord's favor has come"* (NLT).

Jesus focused on accomplishing His God-given mission, which was to adjust our relationship toward God, bringing us back in right standing with the Father. This mission involved the work of justification.

Jesus performed miracles and preached the gospel but, most importantly, He did what He saw the Father do or what He was instructed by the Father to do, not what He wanted to do (John 6:38, 14:31; Matthew 26:39). When Jesus was tempted in the wilderness by the devil, He could have misused His power. Instead, He resisted the devil using the Word of God (Matthew 4:1-11). He remained submitted to the will of the Father.

The works that Jesus performed didn't cease when He left the earth, nor did they cease upon the death of the apostles. That's what a mantle anointing is all about – the works of the throwers continue through catchers from one generation to another.

The promise of 'signs' that follow believers is for you and me, and as many as the Lord God will call (Joel 2:28-29; Acts 2:17-18; Mark 16:17-18). The same power that raised Jesus Christ from the dead lives inside of us.

Whether a thrower or a catcher, we understand that *"...It is not by force nor by [human] strength, but by my Spirit, says the Lord of Heaven's Armies"* (Zechariah 4:6, NLT; brackets added).

The works God wants us to do can only be done through the aid of His Spirit. God has breathed into us power and anointing – power that no one else can supply or take away. Praise God! This powerful mantle anointing must be utilized regularly and not reserved for some special occasion, time, or purpose. Look around you. There's always something to do for the Lord, someone to reach for the Lord. We should be walking in this anointing daily. We can have displays of the demonstration of the Spirit's power, such as was exhibited in the lives of the apostles. The word *"display"* is not used to imply that the anointing is something we should flaunt to gain attention or use as we please without any regard or subjectivity whatsoever to God. On the contrary, we should yield and submit ourselves to God in such a way that He won't hesitate to demonstrate His power in and through us.

Wearing Versus Maintaining

Wearing a mantle anointing and maintaining it are two different things. We already know that wearing the anointing is not just possessing it but functioning in it. Whose job, then, is it to maintain the anointing that we have? It's our job! To maintain something means that it must be treated and kept up in a particular manner in order to preserve it. For example, maintaining a car involves making sure there is gas in the tank, checking the air pressure in the tires every now and then, getting oil changes and tire rotations, tune-ups, and other maintenance work as needed. We, too, should do whatever it takes to maintain the anointing God has deposited in us.

Paul admonishes us in Ephesians 5:18 to be *filled* with the Spirit, which is one of the ways that we wear the mantle anointing of Jesus Christ, allowing His Spirit to fill us completely. Being filled is unlike a half-filled glass of liquid. This filling is like a glass overflowing. God wants us to have excess to pour out to others.

Like a car needs to be maintained, so does the anointing in us because we are human. If we practice maintenance disciplines regularly and sincerely, we will maintain *that* special anointing, and *that* anointing will grow, becoming greater in us. We will experience an increase for the cause of Christ!

In the parable of the talents, the boss gave each of his workers a certain amount of talents based on their ability. To one servant, he gave only one talent. His expectation was that they all would invest their talents, causing them to multiply. The servant who received one talent did nothing with it except hide it. The boss got angry with him because he did nothing to multiply the talent he had received. The servant didn't even put it in the bank! As a result of this act of fearful negligence, the servant's one talent was taken away from him and given to the one with ten talents (Matthew 25:14-28).

God is gracious; at the same time, it offends and hurts Him when He sees us neglecting the anointing which He has given to us. The Holy Spirit is an inner garment whose work takes place on the inside and can be seen [noticed, recognized] through what it produces in us outwardly.

God's way is changing an individual on the inside first, and that change will eventually manifest outwardly. The true essence of an individual is the 'inner person.' Thus, God made a Spirit-to-spirit connection with us.

He especially enjoys those who go all out and take risks to use their talents, like in the parable. God wants to see our willingness in what we do more than what we say. He knows one of the ways we will grow and become better at what we do is by utilizing what He has equipped us with. When we rise to do the work of the Father, we rise in *His* power and might!

The mantle anointing of the Holy Spirit is a promise – a sure thing. Jesus included us as partakers in this promise when He prayed for all those who would believe in Him (John 17:20-22).

The Holy Spirit's mantle is a symbol of our authority, so let us put on His mantle!

Chapter 15: Mantle Anointing and Kingdom Building ~ The Power of Two

The number 2 (two) speaks of establishment and symbolizes agreement. In the Bible, God sent messages twice, gave the same dreams twice, used figures and symbols in twos, and called certain people by name twice. For example, Samuel, Samuel (I Samuel 3:10), Moses, Moses (Exodus 3:4) and Saul, Saul (Acts 9:4).

There's always an advantage in having two work together, over one. Two can get more accomplished. Some people are not comfortable delegating tasks. They feel that in order for a particular task to be done right, they must do it themselves. That holds true at times, especially if there's a breakdown in communication between two people working together or there's some type of dysfunction or uncertainty about the task at hand.
I'm referring to those who absolutely won't delegate no matter what. Where kingdom building is concerned – as it relates to a mantle anointing – two is always better than one. There's power in twos!

Let us look at what the Bible teaches about twos.
Two are better than one because they have a more satisfying return for their labor; for if either of them falls, the one will lift up his companion. But woe to him who is alone when he falls and does not have another to lift him up. Again, if two lie down together, then they keep warm; but how can one be warm alone? (Ecclesiastes 4:9-12, AMP). *In the mouth of two or three witnesses every word may be established* (Matthew 18:16, KJV). *Take one or two others with you and go back again, so that everything you say may be confirmed by two or three witnesses* (Matthew 18:16, NLT).

Denying the spoken words or actions of another is difficult to do when witnesses are present. If only one person witnessed the words or actions, then the person at fault could easily lie or deny the accusation and probably get away with it. Having two or more credible witnesses to testify against the one being accused makes it very difficult for an individual to deny the accusations or convince others to take his or her defense. A charge is more sufficiently substantiated when there's more than one witness. Thus, we see the power of two (or more).

When God showed Joseph the same dream twice about his family submitting to him, it meant that the thing was established; it was going to happen! (See Genesis 37:5-11, 45:1-7).

The number 2 (two) symbolizes agreement, amongst a few other things.

"Can two people walk together without agreeing on the direction? (Amos 3:3, NLT).

Again, I say unto you, that if two of you shall agree on earth as touching anything that they shall ask, it shall be done for them of my Father which is in heaven" (Matthew 18:19, KJV).

"For where two or three gather together because they are mine, I am there among them" (Matthew 18:20, NLT).

"Someone might be able to beat up one of you, but not both of you. As the saying goes, 'A rope made from three strands of cord is hard to break'" (Ecclesiastes 4:12, CEV).

The message is two can do more! In kingdom building we need the power of two. If two can do so much, then just imagine what can happen when there are more than two.

For example, Jesus sent out seventy-two *other* disciples in two groups, paired up in twos (Luke 10:1).

This example reminds us that Jesus had many disciples that were not a part of His original inner circle, yet their devotion, commitment, and loyalty to Him was equal to that of the original twelve. The mission of the seventy-two disciples was a planned campaign to cover more territory. These disciples would be able to reach more people than Jesus and His twelve disciples could reach. Pairing up in twos also ensured that no one would be alone while evangelizing. That's wisdom!

Jesus knew many souls needed to be saved; He recognized His limitations (Luke 10:2). Therefore, Jesus maximized His potential by using people resources to reach those souls. The seventy-two disciples were charged with the responsibility of presenting the gospel and healing the sick (Luke 10:9-10). As the disciples went out, they were given power and authority. Furthermore, Jesus let them know that whoever received their message received it as if it were coming from His own mouth (Luke 10:16).

Matthew 6:33 reads, *"But more than anything else, put God's work first and do what he wants. Then the other things will be yours as well"* (CEV). In other words, we must seek those things that will further God's kingdom and align with His will, and if we do that, the material needs of life will be given to us.

Understanding kingdom building is necessary as it relates to mantle anointing relationships, which are unique to kingdom building. The first thing we need to understand about kingdom building is the kingdom itself and how it operates.

A kingdom is an undivided territory that's subject to a king or monarch – a priestly nation or state. The latter part of this description is exactly how God describes us – we are a kingdom of priests! (See I Peter 2:9-10). Furthermore, we are citizens of the Kingdom of God. Citizenry is part of our identity (Philippians 3:20; Luke 10:20). Since a kingdom is an undivided territory, we can't be entirely successful in kingdom building while there are divisions and barriers among us.

Division blocks resources, rendering us ineffective. The Bible teaches that every kingdom, city, or house divided against itself will not stand. Division is an outgrowth of carnality (Matthew 12:25; I Corinthians 3:2-3).

Kingdom building is a collective effort, meaning there's no room for division or separatism. Let's look at what the book of Nehemiah teaches us on unity as we work for God.

"And they said, 'Let us rise up and build. So, they strengthened their hands for this good work'" (Nehemiah 2:18b, KJV). Two things are evident in this verse. First, to effectively carry out God's will, we must change our posture spiritually and naturally. We must rise up spiritually just as we would physically rise up out of a chair. 'Rising' speaks of a readiness to do something. Only in our eagerness to move forward with the work of God can we accomplish His will. Notwithstanding, it would be helpful for us to understand that we'll not always be inclined to rise up, depending on the task that's set before us. Some things take a lot more effort than others, and it's those things that we need a strong will or desire to do.

Nehemiah 4:6 reads, *"So we rebuilt the wall till all of it reached half its height, for the people worked with all their heart"* (NIV).

In other words, the people had a will, desire to rebuild the wall. We need to pray and ask God for a mind [will, desire] to work.

Understanding the task and the need for it, knowing how God sees us in relation to the task, and how we see ourselves in relation to the task are helpful in rising to the task. Furthermore, we must know and understand what our specific role is and have an expected outcome that's measurable. If we always had it easy, then we would likely slack up and wouldn't appreciate having to work hard to achieve what we want in life. On the contrary, when we can't see our way clearly, God uses this time as an opportunity to develop us through our dependence on Him. Accordingly, we're able to rise to the task, appreciating the time and effort we put into it to get a satisfactory result.

Second, in Nehemiah 2:18, the people recognized that God's work was a good work. It was good because it focused on rebuilding the wall surrounding Jerusalem back to its original intended state. Through this restoration process, God realigned His people, causing them to re-focus on the things that were important to Him, such as cooperating with each other.

Seeing things in proper perspective helps us to recognize and receive the various tasks God has placed before us, enabling us to get started on them. For example, in the book of Nehemiah, the people recognized and appreciated God's goodness. Such recognition is vital if we're going to move forward to do what God has called us to. Sometimes we have wrong ideas about God and His intentions for us. This misperception of God affects how we go about doing His business. Being assured that God's goodness is always present even when we don't see or feel it is huge in accomplishing His mission, especially since understanding the mission is vital to kingdom building.

Regarding mission, the underlying message found throughout the gospel of Mark is that doing *the* mission is what makes us whole or complete. Jesus' mission was to call sinners to repentance. True repentance is restorative to *sinners*. Jesus' role in leading others to repentance made Him complete because He fulfilled what He was sent to do (John 9:4-5). Gratefulness unto God overshadows us when we accomplish what He has called and sent us to do.

The Kingdom Itself

The church is a part of the manifestation of the Kingdom of God in this world. Yet, the Kingdom of God is bigger than our church structures. In fact, kingdom building has very little to do with church structure and denominations, for that matter. It supersedes both! Putting on programs and serving within the four walls of the church are not necessarily kingdom building. Programs provide opportunities for personal and spiritual growth, fellowship, and, in some cases, entertainment.

Kingdom building is not necessarily ministering to each other. The Bible teaches that we assemble together to be edified and perfected for the work of the ministry – working the ministry is kingdom building! (See Ephesians 4:11-15). Kingdom building involves extending oneself outside of the kingdom to bring others into *that* kingdom.

We advance God's Kingdom by helping others find their way inside. The necessary condition of entry into God's Kingdom is that one repents and believes the good news, which means we can't dictate who is part of the kingdom and who isn't. God will do the separating (Romans 10:9-11; Mark 1:15; Matthew 13:30, 47-48).

The church's specific responsibility is equipping members to serve in ways that builds God's Kingdom – those ways are mostly outside of the four walls of the church. The first thing that needs to happen in terms of preparation is having a revelation of who Jesus is because until then, we won't fully understand kingdom building. Comprehension goes beyond just knowing Jesus as Lord and Savior, having died to save the lost. Knowing that the Kingdom of God was ushered in through the earthly ministry of Jesus Christ is a fuller comprehension! For this reason, Jesus stated, *"...the Kingdom of Heaven is near."* What He meant by this was that the Kingdom of God had come because He [Jesus] had come (Matthew 4:17).

God has appointed us kings and priests in His Kingdom to direct, control, and govern as chief officers. We have been set apart for the ministry of the gospel. Because our identity is in Christ, we don't have to identify ourselves with great preachers or singers – for example – or even with the spiritual gifts the Lord has given us. Our identity is not tied to people. It's useless for us to try to establish our own righteousness. This type of identification with people and things was the problem that existed with the Corinthian saints, hindering them from working for God. (See I Corinthians 3:4-7, 9; Romans 10:3; Philippians 2:13).

Since we inhabit God's Kingdom, we must submit to Him and surrender to the control of His government. Kingdom building thrives on our obedience to God. Our human government doesn't run the Kingdom of God; it's operated by the supreme administration of God Himself. Therefore, the Kingdom of God is the government of God (Isaiah 9:7). In God's government, we are expected to exercise authority, giving direction and restraint over the actions of the people.

We are kingdom stewards and are expected to manage, regulate, direct, control, restrain, and influence others!

God has given us guardian responsibility, and He expects us to properly manage what has been placed in our care. As Kingdom stewards, we are required to be faithful, trustworthy, and committed (I Corinthians 4:1-2; Luke 12:42).

Our role in kingdom building is to preach [also translated share] the good news and our testimony to everyone, making disciples of all nations (Mark 16:15-16; Matthew 28:19-20). During Jesus' earthly ministry, the Kingdom of God was the focus of His teachings, and He appointed His disciples to proclaim the same message. We, too, must do on earth what God has already established in Heaven. We must do as the Father does.

There is a clear message in Luke 9:2 concerning kingdom building and Jesus' commission to the disciples – Jesus sent them [set them apart] to preach the Kingdom [rule and reign] of God. Getting the word out about the Kingdom of God is also what He commissioned us to do.

Kingdom building focuses on God's work. It's a spiritual endeavor. Jesus made this clear by stating that His Kingdom is not of this world (John 18:36). That means there's no room for the flesh. Operating in the flesh hinders us from making progress in kingdom building. A rule in kingdom building is that we can't accomplish spiritual things having a carnal mind. On the contrary, we can achieve a lot for God by co-operating with Him (I Corinthians 3:9; II Corinthians 6:1).

In kingdom building, we must build on the same foundation that has already been laid – Jesus Christ (I Corinthians 3:10-11). We are not supposed to be doing anything strange, and we must be cautious when we see others doing things that have no scriptural base or foundation, connecting those things to Jesus Christ.

In Isaiah 43:19, the Lord says, *"See, I am doing a new thing! Now it springs up; do you not perceive it?"* (NIV), but new doesn't mean strange. Stay away from 'strange fire.'

To say the least, kingdom building requires a concentrated effort on our part.

Desire: A Vital Element of Kingdom Building

Let's look again at Nehemiah to learn about desire. Nehemiah and his workers changed their posture by recognizing that God's work was good. Such recognition gave them a desire to do the work. It's difficult to get one's desire back once it's gone. Desire is what fuels us with energy and motivation. Desire drives us, and without it, we can't go forward. Moreover, without desire, we will quit before the job is completed and, in some cases, before the job gets started! It's a terrible thing to lose godly and good desires. As members of the body of Jesus Christ, we need to pray and ask God to put the right desires back in our hearts because absence of it hinders us – individually and collectively – from moving forward.

Discouragement kills desire. Discouragement has three primary sources, but they're not the only sources. I learned in seminary that the three primary sources are lack of relaxation, frustration, and intimidation. Discouragement is one of Satan's most powerful tools against the people of God. If discouragement isn't disbanded in its early stage but, instead, is allowed to fester, it will grow until it turns into other things – lack of desire being one of them. Let's be clear that discouragement doesn't just crop up on its own; many factors lead to it.

Let's turn our attention to some of the other sources of discouragement.

Source One: An Attack Against the Mind

One of the enemy's primary motives against the body of Christ is to get us in a state of mind in which we find it difficult, or are unable, to relax mentally. Being in an un-relaxed state affects us emotionally, spiritually, and physically. The opposite of relaxation is tension, uneasiness, being on edge, and being easily angered. An individual who is unrelaxed doesn't think as clearly as he or she would if relaxed. His or her better judgment is more likely to become clouded during times of tension and stress. In this state, the enemy can easily take advantage of him or her. When we're unrelaxed, we tend to over-react about things and behave impulsively. Additionally, we tend to misinterpret or misjudge what happens to us in a given situation and what others say to us and think of us. Remaining in an unrelaxed state of mind eventually leads to a lack of confidence, instability, and, ultimately, discouragement.

Source Two: An Attack Against the Work

Being frustrated is one of the worst things one can experience. Frustration will cause an individual to abandon a task right in the middle of it or quit altogether without giving it a good try. Frustration comes about when we see the obstacles in a task rather than the opportunities.

Some have encountered very harmful, adverse, or discouraging situations, which has caused us to lose sight of the opportunities, making it more challenging to keep a positive frame of mind. Frustration is an irritator and agitator. When we experience either one of these negative emotions, we can become closed-minded to those things that can help get us through the situation or will help us make the best of the problem. In all of this, God wants us to learn something from what we encounter.

Learning also has to do with being able to identify and take advantage of what the opportunities are in the midst of our challenges.

Frustration is an attack against the completion of an assignment. We can see this motive from its outcomes – quitting, giving up, or abandoning a task.

Source Three: An Attack Against the Call, Office, or Position

The devil uses intimidation as a source of discouragement against us. Those who have purposed in their heart and mind to please God are targets for the enemy. Nonetheless, we don't have to be afraid because the Greater One lives on the inside, and we have His protection. We need to recognize that the enemy also works through people, not only circumstances. When others see us as a threat, they *may* try to intimidate us, to cause us to give in, quit, or abandon the task.

Intimidation causes people to step out of the place God meant for them to be in and get among those they have no business being around. That was Elijah's predicament when he received word that Jezebel was going to kill him for killing the prophets of Baal (I Kings 19). That was David's predicament as Saul pursued him to kill him (I Samuel chapters 27 through 30). David was afraid of Saul to the degree that he went into Philistine territory [Gath] to live and even pledged his loyalty to the Philistine army that he would join them in battle against Saul and Israel.

If we step out of the place we're intended to be in, we run the risk of being in dangerous territory and, thereby, we find ourselves compromising what we believe and know to be right by God's standards. Intimidation can cause us to sell out.

Recognizing that discouragement kills desire is one thing. We need to know what we can do to nurture desire, so discouragement doesn't consume it or us. We can nurture desire through repentance, recognizing God's goodness, and having a good support network.

Let's look at each one in detail.

Repentance

When we're honest with ourselves that we have grown discouraged and that it has caused us to cease from doing God's work, we must repent. True repentance puts us back in right standing with God, relaying to Him that we're willing to forsake our current stance or actions in order to accomplish His will, being assured that through repentance we will find rest in God.

Repentance is not apologizing; there's a difference. We can apologize over things we're caught doing or words spoken and heard by others that are wrong or harmful out of a guilty conscience. The problem with this is often, when the dust settles, we can find ourselves right back in the same position. Think about it. You only need to be honest with yourself and God. How many times have you so-called repented about something that really was only an apology to God because you felt guilty? How many times have you repented – apologized – about the same thing repeatedly? Repentance is not apologizing.

Repentance means forsaking, period. Matthew 3:8 and Acts 26:20 admonish us to bring to God the fruit acceptable for repentance. If our attitude about repentance is insincere, then God won't accept it. I know that sounds harsh, but it's true. Our approach to God must not be phony or hypocritical.

Repentance must be more than lip service; there must be a genuine change of heart and mind, which will be evident in the way we think, act, speak, and live thereafter.

Recognize God's Goodness

We should all recognize that God is good and then work to find His goodness in the situations at hand. The goodness of God leads to repentance (Romans 2:4). Recognizing God's goodness is a sure remedy for discouragement. According to Matthew 7:7-8, we can find God's goodness by asking, seeking, and knocking. There are times when we fail to see God's goodness for being overwhelmed by our daily responsibilities, and we can only see as far as the moment we're in. That's when we should ask God to show us His goodness. If we persistently look for God, we will find that He is with us even when it seems like He's far away. He promised never to leave nor forsake us (Hebrews 13:5).

Support Network

Another remedy for discouragement is having a good support network of loving and godly friends and family who recognize when we have grown discouraged and are willing to help lift us out of that state.

These are just some of the ways we can nourish desire. Nehemiah and his workers had desire; that's what fueled them to complete the work. *"So, the wall was finished..."* (Nehemiah 6:15, KJV). Desire helps us in moving forward even when we don't know where our resources will come from. Desire will help us to continue 'building the wall' – whatever that wall is – while others around us buckle under pressure and the negative influences of others. God's work must be completed. When one task is finished, there'll always be more work to be done.

Kingdom Building: The Mission and The Vision

Another aspect of kingdom building relates to the mission of the one we are working for. In kingdom building, understanding the mission and setting goals for accomplishing that mission are important. Anything less than adequate preparation makes doing the task effectively unattainable.

The mission of a particular task gives us foresight, helping us to understand precisely what's required of us. Therefore, we can look at the mission as the connecting agent to the actual vision of a particular thing, which means kingdom builders need to be visionaries.

According to the American Dictionary of the English Language, a visionary is one who is disposed [set in order] to receive impressions on the imagination. A vision is something imagined to be seen, though not real.

Visionaries receive impressions on the imagination [mind]. We often relate or connect a vision to that which is perceived in the spirit [heart], but visions relate to the imagination. The mind is where God shows us the image of what He wants to do through us. Additionally, God gives us step-by-step instructions for carrying out the vision. Therefore, the vision must be received in the imagination first before becoming a part of the spirit [heart]. By the time the vision reaches our spirit, we would have already received and processed it in our imagination.

When God gives a vision, it doesn't have to be something entirely new. The vision may have some connection to something that already exists – whether presently or from the past.

If we're to be honest, many of us want to forget about our past, especially if it wasn't pleasant or positive, but vision comes from where we have been as well as where we're going. Success, in part, comes from looking at one's past, which then gives motivation and determination for working towards a brighter future.

Understanding that our past has to do with our culture – or what's referred to as a mental model in the business world – is principal. Our mental model allows us to see visions. Vision ties into culture – background, environment in which one was raised, and beliefs. Yet, our cultural background doesn't mean that the outcome of our vision will be restricted to what we know or have experienced according to *that* culture. On the contrary, we can't fully understand where we are going unless we remember and appreciate where we have been (those memorials spoken about earlier). Where we have been should motivate us to move forward to where we are going.

Looking back should always create a desire to go forward in a better way. Those of us who have been redeemed from the past know we're not subject [confined or limited] to our past. Still, we should keep in mind that our past experiences – positive and negative – can give us motivation toward the future without subjecting us to re-live the past. Thank God for Jesus' redeeming power!

Redemption is all about readjusting, re-aligning, and re-dedicating. In a sense, it represents wholeness not so much because we are whole but because the One who redeemed us is perfectly whole.

We can border on discouragement, impatience, and frustration when we don't get positive, instantaneous results in our lives.

We need to remember that change is a process and it takes time. Perhaps the manifestation of change has not yet come to fruition. Change is all around us; we don't always see or feel it, but change is happening. The issue is whether we are inclined to change. If we're inclined to change, then we must be willing to adapt to change as God orchestrates it.

We can't be full of vision without being provoked by that vision. In other words, a vision can be burdensome because it speaks of that which touches the core of our being – something that we desire to be fulfilled, implemented, or changed.

Two Old Testament prophets serve as good examples with regards to their vision and their burden for it. They are Habakkuk and Nehemiah. Both prophets had a vision and were troubled by that vision to the point that they sought God for instruction and guidance. They wanted to know how to move forward with the vision, including who to involve in working towards its fulfillment.

Christian believers should at least have one natural [earthly] vision [goal] and one spiritual vision. The Bible teaches that the absence of vision causes us to be without guidance and direction (Proverbs 29:18). In other words, the absence of prophetic vision or revelation causes us to do as we please. Absence of vision is like being without spiritual guidance. We still need prophetic revelation [utterance] – revelation that will be communicated from God into our imagination. Receiving this kind of revelation ensures that we have the vision God wants us to have, not our own.

Every church's corporate mission should, in some way, equip its members to effectively communicate on the rule and reign of God, so that others can understand and become a part of the Kingdom of God.

With the corporate mission, we must ensure that we are, in fact, kingdom building and not self-building. Self-building is having our own personal agendas that don't align with what God wants us to do and distracts us and others from God's work.

Voices and Kingdom Building

Kingdom building is a divine mission. Our love for God and commitment to Him should be the driving force of kingdom building. Knowing the voice of God is vital as we war with many 'voices' currently that are contrary to God, trying to confuse us.

In John 10:3-5, Jesus said, *"The gatekeeper opens the gate for him, and the sheep recognize his voice and come to him. He calls his own sheep by name and leads them out. After he has gathered his own flock, he walks ahead of them, and they follow him because they know his voice. They won't follow a stranger; they will run from him because they don't know his voice"* (NLT).

The illustration of the sheep and the shepherd shows us the unique relationship that exists between them. First, the [good] shepherd looks out for the best interest of the sheep – he won't allow anything or anyone to harm them. In fact, a good shepherd would rather endure punishment, pain, and suffering rather than allow his sheep to suffer (II Samuel 24:17).

The shepherd establishes a relationship with the sheep to such a degree that the sheep trusts him. Based on this trust, the sheep listens only to the shepherd's instructions, receiving guidance. They hear the voice of others but only recognize the uniqueness of their shepherd's voice; thus, obeying that voice.

Like sheep, we should be cautious about who we seek advice from. In II Chronicles 10:6-15, Rehoboam rejected advice from the elders [older counselors] and, instead, asked the opinion of the young men who had grown up with him – his peers. Their bad advice led to rebellion against leadership and government. This teaches us that seeking advice from friends or peers *may* not always be the best move, especially if they don't have the mind of Christ, even though they may call themselves Christians.

We are the sheep of His pasture. Jesus is the Good Shepherd. He has called *some* individuals into mantle anointing relationships on a person-to-person basis. More importantly, we have all been called into a mantle anointing relationship with the Holy Spirit. The thing that's most helpful in knowing and recognizing God's voice above all other voices is discernment. Discernment is the ability to distinguish what's real and what isn't. It's the ability to decipher truth from error, knowing the difference in what's being communicated by knowing the motive of the communicator. One of the ways we can grow in discerning God calling us into mantle anointing relationships is through prayer.

An individual can effectively work towards building the Kingdom of God with the proper tools in hand. There are nine kingdom keys that we should utilize to help us successfully build God's Kingdom.

Let's take a brief look at what they are.

Kingdom Key #1: The Power of Agreement

The concept of two being more productive than one takes effect under this kingdom key. Remember, two is the number of establishment and it symbolizes agreement (Matthew 18:19-20).

We should practice what the Bible teaches – touching and agreeing. The sincere agreement of two people in prayer for the same purpose – in accordance with God's Word and will – is powerful enough to move God on their behalf.

Kingdom Key #2: The Power of Sacrifice

According to the American Dictionary of the English Language, to sacrifice is to destroy, surrender, or suffer to be lost for the sake of obtaining something; to devote with loss. A good scriptural example of sacrificing is found in Matthew 19:12, which talks about those who choose not to marry for the sake of kingdom building. The decision not to marry *can be* a sacrifice in and of itself for some people. The issue is not whether such individuals shouldn't marry because of a lack of desire but, instead, they choose not to marry because something else is more important with high priority to them. Putting God and the needs of others before one's own needs and desires – and doing so well – is true sacrifice!

Kingdom Key #3: The Power of Faith

Faith is hope. Hope is belief or trust in something or someone. The Bible teaches us that everyone needs faith – saving faith to receive God (Hebrews 11:6). Saving faith doesn't come about as a result of being a Christian; neither is it just for Christians. Saving faith works in sinners; it's this kind of faith that brings people to Christ. The power of faith is different than saving faith; it has to do with faith that grows [matures, increases] and performs [produces] in accordance with our relationship with God.

The power of faith produces, causing the intangible, invisible thing to materialize, yet it doesn't wait on proof but rejoices when the proof comes.

In other words, faith's power doesn't get its energy, excitement, or enthusiasm from seeing the proof. It is energized and grows stronger in expectancy in the absence of proof, knowing that at the right time, proof will manifest.

Kingdom Key #4: The Power of Binding and Loosing

We are equipped to bind and loose since we hold the keys of the kingdom. Keys are a symbol of authority, giving access (Matthew 16:19, 18:18). Whatever we bind [render inactive and ineffective] in the earthly realm is bound in the heavenly realm, and whatever we loose [release, call into being with scripture as our base] in the earthly realm is loosed in the heavenly realm. We must utilize this kingdom key in our homes, churches, schools, jobs, and communities.

Kingdom Key #5: The Power of Confession or Profession

When Jesus asked the disciples what they thought about Him, Simon Peter replied, *"...Thou art the Christ, the Son of the living God."* (Matthew 16:13-19, KJV). Peter's confession reflected that the revelation knowledge had come from God. What he confessed wasn't learned from any human being. As kingdom builders, we, too, must seek God for revelation knowledge so that we'll confess that which is insightful and liberates others.

The power of confession has to do with ordering our words to align with what God says, so they'll produce godly results. Our confession has the power to produce. Therefore, we must be careful what we say! (See Proverbs 18:21; Matthew 12:37).

Kingdom Key #6: The Power of Authority

We have delegated authority – the right to tap into our power source – the Holy Spirit – to destroy Satan's works (Luke 10:19; Psalm 60:12). We can do so through the power of authority given to us by Jesus Christ. Our authority as believers won't work if we reserve it, not utilizing it. Power isn't given unless there's a need for it. Power is used to resist and oppose contrary forces; it's not used against friends or allies. We have been given power and authority to resist the enemy. Power of authority is useless without an enemy. We can't be afraid to use the authority God has given us over the enemy.

Kingdom Key #7: The Power of Possessing a Warrior's Mentality

We are soldiers in the army of the Lord. Soldiers are expected to be brave, engage in military life, endure hardships and sufferings. In II Timothy 2:3-4, Paul admonished Timothy to endure suffering as a good soldier and, as Christ's soldier, not to allow himself to become tied up in the affairs of life because that would prevent him from satisfying Christ, the one who enlisted him in His army (I Timothy 1:18-19; Hebrews 10:32-36; I Timothy 6:12; Ephesians 6:12-13). A soldier is a warrior who is responsible for tearing down strongholds and taking them captive! (See II Corinthians 10:3-5). We can do so in full armor!

Kingdom Key #8: Divide and Conquer

As warriors, we have the ability – through the Holy Spirit – to walk away from battles with spoils from the enemy rather than allowing him to take [steal] from us. Victorious endings are portrayed in many of the Old Testament scriptures on physical combat.

For example, in II Chronicles 20:25, Jehoshaphat and his men went out to gather the plunder [spoil] after they had fought the enemy. They found vast amounts of equipment, clothing, and other valuables – more than they could carry. There was so much spoil that it took them three days just to collect it all! The word *"plunder"* means to spoil and to take the goods of an enemy by open force. Other scriptures on taking spoil include: Genesis 14:12, 14-16; Exodus 12:36; I Samuel 14:32; 17:53; II Chronicles 14:13; 15:11; I Chronicles 26:27; II Samuel 3:22; II Kings 7:16.

Spiritual warfare poses a threat of losing something when we try to fight in our own strength or when we're unprepared for battle. Ephesians 6 describes the kind of warfare we will encounter, telling us how to dress (II Corinthians 10:3-5). In the same way, when we fight with God's power, we come out of battles having gained something valuable rather than suffering loss. Moreover, when we allow God to teach us how to fight each battle, we learn how the devil plots and schemes, and we're better equipped.

In warfare, our spiritual senses are heightened, and what's meant to harm us aids in strengthening us. These are examples of the kinds of spoils being referred to – not necessarily materialistic spoils. Demonically inspired attacks can work for our advantage because, through them, God can open doors of opportunities and bestow blessings upon us. Just look at Mordecai in the Book of Esther and Joseph in the Book of Genesis and Job in the Book of Job.

As warriors, we're triumphant because of what God has done on our behalf – through His Son, Jesus Christ – and we can overcome opposition.

Kingdom Key #9: Kingdom Prayer

Kingdom prayer is praying for the interest of God's Kingdom. A key element in kingdom prayer is the power of intercession.

We can run interference in the spirit realm through the Holy Spirit, our Intercessor (Romans 8:26, 27, 34; I Timothy 2:1). Our prayers would be ineffective without the aid of the Holy Spirit, but through Him, we can interrupt and cancel the enemy's plans. We should take advantage of leaning on our Intercessor in prayer, so our prayers will work!

The kingdom keys provided are brief in the descriptions, but hopefully they provide clear explanations of what each kingdom key does. Let's use these kingdom keys daily.

If this book has blessed you in any way, kindly leave a professional, positive review on Amazon.com ~ thank you!

Chapter 16: Execution of a Mantle Anointing

According to The Merriam-Webster Concise Dictionary, the word *"execute"* means to carry to completion; to perform; to produce in accordance with a plan or design. To execute under a mantle anointing is to perform, produce, or carry out a particular task or assignment. There are three important stages that must be completed prior to an individual arriving at the execution stage. The three stages are: recognition, identification, and studying. Let's look at each stage.

Stage One: Recognition

An individual can't take part in a mantle anointing relationship without recognizing that he or she has been called to such a relationship. Keywords that describe the word *"recognition"* are perceive clearly, realize, and acknowledge. Recognition, then, speaks of a special awareness – one that causes an individual to take notice or give special attention to something. An individual who notices something to this degree has, more than likely, set his or her undivided attention on that thing to pursue it.

Those who are in mantle anointing relationships, embracing what recognition embodies, are ready to move on to stage two, the identification stage.

Stage Two: Identification

During this stage, mentees model the thought-pattern and actions as observed in their mentor. The keyword in this stage is *"model,"* which means mentees imitate their mentor.

Mentees can't complete the identification stage without coming into agreement with their mentor, modeling that person for the sole purpose of continuing a particular task. When mentees get to this point, they are ready to move on to the third stage, studying.

Stage Three: Studying

In this stage, studying or observing the life and work of the mentor is especially important on the part of the mentee. The studying stage is more intense than in the first two stages. Being involved in mantle anointing relationships without knowing the style and work of the mentor isn't prudent. In this stage, the possibility of surprises cropping up in the relationship or unrecognizable signs between the two should be minimal, if at all.

The mentee should take full advantage of observing the mentor in great detail. Observing includes asking questions to gain an understanding and for general knowledge, clarity, and enlightenment. Nothing is too small or minute to take notice of. Mentees must study their mentor thoroughly so they can become familiar with the execution-style of their mentor as theirs *may* be similar in certain ways.

As emphasized in previous chapters, following and serving on the part of the mentee are necessary during the studying stage. Greater emphasis is placed on mentees in terms of their responsibilities because of the training and equipping needed in preparation of the execution stage. The mentor is already in execution mode.

Mentees should have or be given plenty of opportunities for hands-on-training or times to practice. This is one of the most important aspects in successfully and effectively executing under a mantle anointing.

Jesus mentored His disciples before releasing them. He taught them daily, taking them along with Him as He went out to do the work of the Father, so they could observe. The ability to observe so that one learns is an acquired skill. Observation is not a skill that is developed overnight and it comes easier for some. With consistent practice, one can master the skill of observation, which involves intake and output.

A vital role on the part of mentors is to observe their mentees to measure progress and growth. Mentors must watch their apprentices to know what they can handle and take an active part in giving them tasks, feedback, and instructions.

Observing takes discipline and patience. Mentees can become eager to move to execution mode and grow impatient with observing, especially when they know they can do a particular task. There's always something to be learned through observation on the part of both mentors and mentees. Being open-minded, then, is critical during the studying stage. Additionally, being eager to learn is a good trait to possess, but there must be discipline with regards to control, proper balance, and maintenance, so that zeal doesn't get mentees off on a bad start.

Mentees who are eager to learn want to be present whenever there's an opportunity for learning. They will sit attentively asking questions when there's space for doing so, which is a form of participation that they may gain something beneficial from the experience.

Elisha did what he saw Elijah do. Elijah used his mantle to divide the waters of the Jordan River, and so did Elisha. What Elisha's mentor did, worked. If it was good enough for Elijah, it was good enough for Elisha (II Kings 2:8, 13-14).

In the present church age, it's tempting for mentees to want to skip the observation stage and move to the execution stage. Consequently, skipping steps can be detrimental *if* mentees don't know what they are doing. In mantle anointing relationships, a lot can be learned from paying careful attention to those who already know the way. One of the ways mentees can develop the skill of observation is by asking their mentor to evaluate them at specific times during a particular stage of the process. The evaluation allows mentees to get regular feedback from their mentor on how well they observed and applied what they observed and where they need to improve. Furthermore, mentees can develop the skill of observation by measuring how well they receive, process, and apply instructions.

Eventually, Jesus released His disciples to practice or execute what they had learned. Even so, Jesus asked His disciples to report back to Him what they had done, which means they were still in the training stage.

The disciples had to understand and embrace Jesus' mission inside, out. Being in the right company was necessary for the disciples as it pertained to their training and preparation. The right company was vital to their developmental stage, as the time would come when they would be sent out and would encounter 'bad' company. In the same way, it's vital that we have the right people-connections as it pertains to our training, preparation, and development.

Having the right people around us helps to keep our surroundings healthy and wholesome. Therefore, we must be careful who we keep company with. First Corinthians 15:33 reads, *"Don't fool yourselves. Bad friends will destroy you"* (CEV).

Proverbs 12:18 reads, *"...the words of the wise bring healing..."* and Proverbs 27:17 reads, *"As iron sharpens iron, a friend sharpens a friend"* (NLT). Wisdom dictates surrounding oneself with faithful people because *"Putting confidence in an unreliable person is like chewing with a toothache or walking on a broken foot"* (Proverbs 25:19, NLT). Those we surround ourselves with will have an effect – good or bad – on how we function in mantle anointing relationships.

Mentees get to flex their spiritual muscles during the execution or practice stage. Mentees should take full advantage of the knowledge, gifting, and experiences of their mentors by asking questions. Doing so ensures that mentees will learn, grow, and be enlightened.

Another aspect that's vital to the execution stage is the separation process. The word *"separation"* means to disunite, to cease to be together. The act of separating isn't always a comfortable feeling, at least not when separating from healthy, wholesome, and beneficial relationships that one *may* not want to separate from. The process certainly can be painful and can be viewed as a time of testing on the part of mentees, proving whether they can stand on their own.

Sometimes we become comfortable knowing we have others to depend on. Only when those individuals are separated from us, do we find out what we're really made up of and how significant others are to our overall growth.

There's a tendency for some people to become attached to others. Healthy attachment isn't wrong in and of itself, but it can make the separation process more painful. Elisha cried out after Elijah and tore his clothes at Elijah's departure (I Kings 2:12).

Separation between those in mantle anointing relationships is inevitable. On the contrary, as Spirit-filled believers, we don't have to worry about being separated from the mantle anointing of the Holy Spirit unless we choose to separate from Him. Jesus promised that He would never leave nor forsake us (Hebrews 13:5).

The mentor has a responsibility to separate from the task when his or her assignment has ended in a particular role, location, or both. It's possible for God to send the mentor to a different location with the same or similar assignment. Moreover, He can promote the mentor to another position but keep him or her in the same location. In this case, the mentee benefits because he or she still has access to the mentor. Although mentors may reach a point where they are no longer involved in carrying out a particular task, the work will be continued because they trained and equipped their mentee with what was needed for continuation and/or expansion.

There came a time when Elijah had to leave Elisha, Moses had to leave Joshua, and Jesus had to physically leave the apostles and disciples. By the time the separation occurred, the mentees – the ones catching the mantle – were equipped, trained in specialized areas, and ready to serve as successors even if they didn't feel fully equipped. In the case of Jesus, those whom He had trained and equipped became an extension of Himself. For *some* involved in mantle anointing relationships, the time will come when they will have to separate from their mentor.

Separation shouldn't cause the mission to be aborted, hindered, or stopped in any way. If separation has an adverse effect on the mission, it could mean something lacked in the actual relationship before it was severed, or the connection was not good to begin with.

In contrast, a definite timeline, smooth transition, and an ongoing process – including goals and objectives for continuing the mission – should exist. By the time mentees reach the execution stage, they should be well-equipped to continue the work. There will be times of uncertainty, doubt, fear, and reluctance. Nevertheless, mentees must reach the execution stage; otherwise, they will be ineffective in their role as successors.

Joshua needed reassurance from God many times in his role as Moses' successor. Thus, God continually encouraged Joshua to have good courage. The disciples, too, were not sure they were ready to continue the work of Jesus Christ until the Holy Spirit came upon them, giving them power – authority, boldness, and courage.

Being well equipped for a specific work doesn't mean an individual can't continue to learn and grow while doing that particular work. In the execution stage, one has the benefit of learning and growing while performing tasks.

God always gives us opportunities to learn, ask questions, and get clear direction and guidance so that we are well informed prior to starting important tasks and filling critical roles. Mentees need to recognize opportunities as they present themselves and take advantage of those opportunities. Not taking advantage of opportunities can be detrimental to the execution of the task once separation from the mentor occurs.

Execution of a mantle anointing is performed with the aid of the Holy Spirit, in the name of the Lord Jesus Christ. Why apply the name of Jesus? We are admonished in scripture to do everything – whether in word or deed – in the name of the Lord Jesus Christ (Colossians 3:17).

David was admirable because when he went out to challenge the Philistine giant, Goliath, in battle, he didn't go representing himself or in his own strength and power. Instead, he acknowledged the Lord as his source – his victor.

"David shouted in reply, you come to me with sword, spear, and javelin, but I come to you in the name of the Lord Almighty—the God of the armies of Israel, whom you [Goliath] have defied" (I Samuel 17:45, NLT).

The key to successfully executing tasks under a mantle anointing is being confident in the one we represent and utilizing the power and authority delegated by that person. We represent the Lord Jesus Christ, wearing His mantle in the person of the Holy Spirit.

There's no greater power or authority that exists than what has been given to the Spirit-filled believer. In contrast, being governed by our own will can make things difficult for us when attempting to execute a task under the mantle anointing of Jesus Christ. When we try to do things in our own strength, we automatically open the door for failure, but when we operate in the power of Christ, we're destined for good success.

Mantle anointing relationships are not only recognized by those involved, they're recognizable by those outside of the relationship – the onlookers. Even so, it's possible for those outside of such relationships to misunderstand what they observe between those involved. Thus, those who don't understand what they see should be careful not to engage in negative and judgmental conversations about such relationships. Their perception *could* be wrong and thereby damaging, especially if it is spread to others.

The connection in mantle anointing relationships is strong. Elisha was always referred to in association with Elijah, Joshua with Moses, Timothy with Paul, and the disciples with Jesus Christ. The association was made because they were together more times than not. One was rarely seen without the other. Mantle anointing relationships are not secretive in nature; they are obvious to the public. Should any be secretive, then something is wrong. For two people to be in a mantle anointing relationship, and the association not be evident to others is quite unusual. Even if those in the relationship are only recognized by others who are in their immediate sphere of influence, they are recognized nonetheless and that's better than nothing. As a side note, beware of those who want to know you intimately privately but shy away from you, acting as if they don't know you publicly. This is a red flag! It could mean their motive for wanting to know you privately is wrong or their association with certain others makes being in relationship with you questionable by those individuals. This is wrong!

"Then Elisha picked up Elijah's cloak and returned to the bank of the Jordan River. He struck the water with the cloak and cried out, 'Where is the Lord, the God of Elijah?' Then the river divided, and Elisha went across. When the group of prophets from Jericho saw what happened, they exclaimed, Elisha has become Elijah's successor! And they went to meet him and bowed down before him" (2 Kings 2:13-15, NLT).

Notice what happened. When the prophets saw Elisha, they knew that what had transpired. In fact, they knew all along what was going to happen as they were prophets of God, and it was made known to them (II Kings 2:7, 15). Elisha as successor and no longer servant was recognizable to them.

Chapter 17: Wrapping One's Face in a Mantle Anointing

"And it was so when Elijah heard it [God's voice] that he wrapped his face in his mantle, and went out, and stood in the entering in of the cave" (I Kings 19:13, KJV; brackets added). Hearing God's voice caused Elijah to get in a state of readiness, moving to the entrance of the cave for further instructions.

We could undoubtedly explore what it meant when Elijah wrapped his face in his mantle. We could say he did so out of fear of or deference for God. We could speculate that maybe the glory of God shined so brightly as he spoke to Elijah that he covered his face. Moreover, we could say that Elijah covered his face out of shame, knowing that he was in hiding. What we know for sure is that at this particular time, Elijah was running from Jezebel, who threatened his life because he had killed all of the prophets of Baal (I Kings 18:40, 19:1-3). Elijah had done the will of God, yet it brought a threat upon his life. There are times when doing the will of God *may* put us in danger of losing our lives or something dear to us – perhaps a career, marriage, or friends. Threatening us is one of the ways the enemy tries to divert us from doing God's will; however, but God is our Champion, and He has never lost a battle.

Before I provide insight on what it means to wrap one's face in a mantle anointing, let's look at the act of wrapping something. Wrapping involves covering something, ensuring that no part of it is exposed or seen. Furthermore, wrapping is a means of protection and preservation. Spiritually, wrapping one's face in a mantle anointing signifies a level of trust that exists between the thrower and catcher, which ultimately causes the catcher to step forward, positioning himself or herself for action and to receive instruction.

The 'entrance of the cave' is the spiritual threshold, which signifies a point or place of beginning, a turning point, or a place in which the Holy Spirit's effect or influence on an individual is revealed to him or her.

When Elijah heard God's voice and stood at the entrance of the cave, he did so because he was influenced by God's presence. Initially, recognition of God's voice brought Elijah to the threshold. God influenced Elijah in a way that produced results. Such an influence was the beginning stage of Elijah getting out of the place of fear and returning to do the work God had called him to. It was a turning point in his life.

Wrapping one's face in a mantle anointing can signify the beginning of something new or a turning point, giving the individual the opportunity to get back on track with God. God is the One we should look to for influence, being assured that it will stimulate us to action!

Let's look at the importance of the face and why we need to wrap our face in a mantle anointing spiritually. The face is the area in which most of our sensory perception parts are located. For example, our eyes, ears, nose, and mouth. These parts serve a vital role or function naturally, and they have spiritual implications.

Eyes

Our eyes allow us to see people, things, movement of people and things, color distinctions, light and darkness. Our eyes give direction and guidance to other body parts – namely the feet – showing them the way. Without eyes, getting around would be difficult.

Our eyes help in the coordination of other members of our body that are also important to the overall function and productivity of the body, such as the hands and feet. For example, one needs to focus his or her eyes on an object – making an initial visual contact – before reaching out his or her hand to pick up that object.

Our eyes also influence what we become naturally and spiritually. For this reason, we should be careful to monitor what we watch, especially as it pertains to television and social media outlets. From a spiritual point of view, look at what Matthew 6:22 says about the eyes. It reads, *"The light of the body is the eye"* (KJV). The New Living Translation reads, *"Your eye is a lamp for your body."* In other words, the eyes are the entranceway to the soul. Sometimes we can get a sense of what a person is thinking or feeling by looking into that person's eyes. There's a difference, however, between natural vision and spiritual vision.

Natural Vision

Natural vision is our capacity to see things, people, shapes, colors, and sizes. Without natural vision or sight, there's darkness in the body because of the inability to see light variations, objects, people, and color distinctions. Simply put, without natural vision, one can't find his or her way around without special accommodations such as the aid of a cane, a service dog or assistance from another person. Otherwise, the person who is blind would grope around trying to find his or her way (Deuteronomy 28:28-29). Most of those who are blind can perceive light, which is very different from seeing light. Perceiving light alone doesn't help with finding one's way around.

There are many people who don't have natural vision, which is called blindness. Some people are born blind like the man spoken of in John 9:1-7.

On the contrary, some people go blind due to certain medical conditions, or their vision becomes impaired as they grow older due to the body's tendency to break down over time.

There's a big difference between a person who is born blind and a person who goes blind through the course of life. Nonetheless, the result is the same for both individuals – they are blind. The life and experience of the person who goes blind is very different from the life of the person who is born blind. It must be very depressing, fearful, and frustrating for an individual who once had eyesight, to lose it. One of the ways we enjoy life is through our ability to see. Being able to see brings pleasure and gratitude to the mind, body, and spirit. We look upon and appreciate God's creation because of our ability to see. Seeing is pleasantly entertaining but it's also sorrowful to behold the bad things that are happening in our world.

Having sight is part of our complete makeup. The person who is born blind can't enjoy his or her surroundings; he or she can only hear about it from others and then use his or her imagination to mentally visualize. The expression that alludes to an individual not missing what he or she has never had is truthful to a degree. In the same way, we were created with an innate awareness to know what's normal as it pertains to the proper functioning of the body. One can't help but to think about how a person who lacks something as important as eyesight feels. Of course, there are those who embrace their blindness and live a very productive, good life. Kudos to them! But perhaps others who are blind thinks about their condition from time to time, wondering what it would be like to have sight. Maybe they hope and pray for a medical breakthrough, miracle, or intervention that would give them sight or restore it. Thank God that with modern technology and medicine, it's possible for sight to be restored. Some sight is undoubtedly better than no sight at all.

When it comes to sleep, which we all need, both sight and blindness affect sleep patterns based on what's taking place in the brain.

The person who goes blind very likely experiences unhappiness, sadness/depression, frustration, and perhaps anger and bitterness because he or she once had eyesight, but that function was damaged. On the contrary, the individual that goes blind has memories of what things look like and can preserve those memories to gain satisfaction in what seems to be an unfortunate situation. Sometimes we don't appreciate what we have until we no longer have it. Only then do we begin to truly reminisce, wishing we had appreciated that thing (or person) while it was ours. Eyesight is a very important function of the human composition. What a blessing it is to have vision!

Spiritual Vision

Spiritual vision is our capacity to see clearly into the things of God. As stated earlier, in the natural realm, some are born without vision, and others lose their sight. In the spiritual realm, those who are born again, have had their spiritual vision corrected, which was out of focus from walking in darkness before accepting Christ. Spiritually, lack of vision speaks of darkness and the Bible teaches that only a fool would choose to live in darkness – enslaved to the sinful nature and not knowing Christ – when he or she could walk in the light of Christ. (See Ecclesiastes 2:14; Psalm 27:1, 36:9; John 8:12, 9:5). The good news is: according to Psalm 18:28, God promised to enlighten our darkness. Moreover, He promised to give light to those that sit in darkness, according to Luke 1:79, which was a prophetic word concerning Jesus Christ (Luke 1:64-80). Notice, Jesus describes Himself in John 8:12 as the *"Light of the world,"* and He tells us in Matthew 5:13-16 that we are both light and salt of the earth.

Spiritual vision or enlightenment comes once an individual is born again (See John 3:7). In other words, he or she receives light when receiving Jesus Christ. That means spiritual vision has nothing to do with natural vision. Born again Christian believers must ensure that they utilize their spiritual vision rather than natural vision for the things of God. Clearly, spiritual vision is only possible through Jesus Christ, the Light Himself.

We all once lacked spiritual vision, but because the Light has come into our hearts, we now have it (Isaiah 60:1-2). Although Isaiah 60:1-2 was a prophetic word to the Jews, we know that they were temporarily blinded because of unbelief so that we – Gentiles, non-Jews – could receive the Light of Christ (Romans 11:17-21, 23-24). Thus, how we shape the mind's eye in relation to spiritual things is imperative. Our eyes should be focused on God for spiritual guidance (Proverbs 3:6).

God speaks to us by giving us insight - wisdom. First Corinthians 2:9-10 speaks of such wisdom, reading *"...What God has planned for people who love him is more than eyes have seen or ears have heard. It has never even entered our minds! God's Spirit has shown you everything. His Spirit finds out everything, even what is deep in the mind of God"* (CEV). I've heard believers quoting verse nine, but not verse ten. Verse ten clearly tells us that God has revealed future things to us by the Holy Spirit. We have insight; it's called revelation!

Vision is tied to the spirit realm, while sight is tied to the natural realm. God enables us – through the Holy Spirit – to envision that which pertains to His will and His expectations of us. To envision something is to look from an internal point of view. To see naturally means to look at something or someone from an external point of view.

John saw a tremendous vision; he had insight (Revelation 1:10-20). His vision was a prophetic one telling him of things to come; thereby, connecting the name of the book – Revelation – to those things that John saw. Revelation has to do with enlightenment and instruction; it reveals that which was hidden, making it plain. The book of Revelation does just that – reveals, enlightens, and instructs.

Simon Peter had insight into all types of beasts on a sheet which God instructed him to eat from. This insight was necessary to prepare Peter to receive and do the work of the Lord. Prior to the vision or insight, Peter was biased bound to Jewish law. Following the vision, he was freed from the things that would have hindered him from ministering to those God had assigned him to (Acts 10:1-45). God was teaching Peter how to accept, relate, interact, and mingle with people different than himself, to minister salvation to them and not only to the Jews. Jesus Christ died for every race!

Now we can better understand how spiritual vision and enlightenment work together. Thank God for spiritual [in]sight!

Ears

The ears are equally as important as the eyes because they allow us to hear sounds and voices, whether in a whisper or a loud tone. Our ears can hear things miles away depending on the sound being carried and the sharpness of our hearing. The ears are so unique to the body that they serve as the equilibrium – balance center of the body – helping to keep the whole body balanced. It is a fact that *sometimes* when dizziness occurs – especially when an individual has a cold – it's because there *may* be an inner ear problem that sets the body off balance, causing an imbalance. The fact that ears – small members – have such an effect on the entire body is amazing!

Our ears help us to process things mentally. As information is received through that organ, it is then internalized through our thought process or mind and leads to some form of outcome. The ear serves a unique purpose spiritually and is critical to us receiving what we need from God. *"If you have ears, listen to what the Spirit says to the churches"* (Revelation 2:11, 17, 29; 3:6, 13, 22, CEV). Hearing involves receiving what's being said and understanding, applying the same, and – depending on the individual's role and when appropriate – conveying the message to others. The importance of application is why James instructs us to be doers of the Word and not hearers only (James 1:22). God speaks mysteries into the ear. At times He speaks forcefully – almost audibly as though another individual is talking – and other times, He speaks softly to the inner person as in the case with Elijah. *"And after the earthquake a fire; but the Lord was not in the fire: and after the fire a still small voice"* (I Kings 19:12, KJV).

God speaks internally to the inner person; the spiritual ear. Jesus – in the book of Mark – conveys to us, through the parable of the sower, the importance of hearing and retaining what we hear. Verse nine reads, *"Then he [Jesus] said, 'Anyone with ears to hear should listen and understand'"* (Mark 4:9, NLT; Brackets added. See also vs 3-23). This verse is repeated in the book of Revelation, chapters two and three. The admonition is precisely the same in both books.

The ability to hear requires an understanding of what's being communicated. We must listen to what the Spirit is saying and perceive what He is speaking to us. That means understanding what the Holy Spirit is saying. From human to human, the inability to hear in the full sense of the word represents, in part, a breakdown in communication either on the part of the hearer or the communicator. From the Holy Spirit to an individual, that breakdown rests solely on the part of the hearer. If a message is not fully understood or heard – especially where action may be required on the part of the hearer – then the task usually doesn't get done or is done incorrectly. Misunderstandings can really cause a mess! Thus, Jesus placed a lot of emphasis on hearing. Hearing in the full sense of the word is vital to experience and achieve growth in both the natural and spiritual realms.

In order to develop good listening skills, one of the first things we must do is be attentive. Attentiveness requires that we be focused on what is being spoken at a particular time and not allow ourselves to become distracted internally or externally. Many of us would agree that it can be very challenging to remain focused when so many things bombard us on a daily basis. Additionally, attentiveness requires one to be in a position of readiness – not getting ready but being ready! Part of being attentive is the ability to apply what we have learned through hearing.

Nose

The nose is our 'scent' detector. Through our nose, we smell pleasant scents, unpleasant scents, delectable scents, recognizable scents, and unrecognizable scents. Certain cold symptoms are expelled from the body through the nose. Most importantly, we breathe through our nose. The nostrils are what God breathed into when he created Adam (Genesis 2:7). Only when God breathed into Adam's nostrils the breath of life did he become a living soul. Prior to this act, Adam simply had a body without life. In the same way spiritually, Jesus Christ breathed into our nostrils the breath of life – the Holy Spirit – and now we are lively stones (I Peter 2:5).

For those who are 'sons of God,' – no gender attached – the nose relates to the scent of Christ in the spiritual realm. Second Corinthians 2:5 reads, *"For we are unto God a sweet-smelling savor of Christ, in them that are saved"* (KJV). Ephesians 5:2 says that because of Christ's love toward us, He gave Himself for us an offering and a sacrifice to God for a sweet-smelling savor.

Through Jesus Christ, we no longer stink in the nostrils of God. When God looks at us, He sees Christ. To take the scent factor to another level, our spiritual smelling or scent speaks of sacrificing that which is pleasing unto God. God desires to smell a sweet-smelling aroma in terms of our worship and praise of Him, as well as our lifestyle as Christian believers.

Mouth

The mouth is the vehicle used to communicate or express one's thoughts and feelings. The Bible speaks about the mouth as housing the most unruly, deadly member of the body – the tongue. James 3:5-6 reads, *"Our tongues are small too, and yet they brag about big things. It takes only a spark to start a forest fire!*

The tongue is like a spark. It is an evil power that dirties the rest of the body and sets a person's entire life on fire with flames that come from hell itself." (CEV). James describes the tongue – out of control – as a fire that's unruly, evil, and full of deadly poison because it kills unmercifully, leaving no trace of life (James 3:8). On the contrary, as a yielding member to the Holy Spirit, the tongue has the ability to do wonderful things such as bless God and others, encourage and say positive things to and about others. Using our tongue in ways that please God and glorifies Him is our responsibility.

The tongue is used in the melodious expression in the form of singing. The entrance to the body and the way the heart expresses itself is through the tongue – mouth. The Bible tells us that out of the abundance of the heart, the mouth speaks (Matthew 12:34). Moreover, the mouth is the vehicle by which food and drink enter the body and one of the ways in which they exit the body.

All our sensory perception parts are important, but the mouth is one of the most important parts. The most powerful tool by which the gospel message is communicated by way of preaching, teaching, singing, sharing, and witnessing is through the mouth and tongue.

God has shown me the importance of the face in the natural realm to communicate a spiritual message: we need to 'wrap our face' in His glory, guarding our sensory perception parts. Just as we do certain things to protect and maintain those parts in the natural realm, we must do so in the spirit realm.

Ways to do so include looking at godly things; listening to godly messages and engaging in godly conversations and having godly friendships; absorbing, embracing and practicing godly truths and disciplines; tasting and proving that the Lord is good as it pertains to spiritual nourishment; and speaking godly words (Psalm 34:1, 8; Ephesians 4:29 and Colossians 3:8).

Chapter 18: The Anointing and Its Diversity

The anointing flows downward from God, working differently in and through each of us. First Corinthians 12:6-7 reads, *"...and we can each do different things. Yet the same God works in all of us and helps us in everything we do. The Spirit has given each of us a special way of serving others"* (CEV). The anointing works through us on different levels. Let's look at what those levels are.

A Double Portion Mantle Anointing

A double portion mantle anointing empowers successors with twice as much ability and/or resources to accomplish a particular task than that of their predecessor. Such was the case with Elijah and Elisha, for example. A double portion anointing is extraordinary and supernatural.

A double portion mantle anointing reinforces what already exists. In other words, there's added strength and durability; it lasts! The kind of strength one acquires under this type of anointing comes with a new force, assistance or support, and strength that brings an increase. Praise God!

Greater Works Mantle Anointing

A greater works mantle anointing is what Jesus promised us according to John 14:12 – it's an empowerment anointing. Jesus has empowered us to do His work, making it possible for us to achieve more wide-spread results – because of our reach – than that which He achieved during his earthly ministry. Jesus wasn't intimidated by the potential of His followers. After all, He trained them, and the servant is not greater than the master.
The greater works mantle anointing – for one – allows us to reach beyond our immediate sphere of influence.

Thus, this kind of an anointing can be understood as an expandable anointing that increases. We can do more in terms of reaching others with the gospel because we have more available resources, helping us to 'touch' the world. During Jesus' earthly ministry, He was geographically and physically limited. Yes, He was both God and man, but He lived His life on earth as a man born of a woman and carried out His mission as a man. If that was not true, then He would have rescued Himself from the wilderness temptations of the devil by calling down angels, and He would have come down from the Cross. Jesus Christ could only be in one place at a time, but today, because of technology and different modes of transportation, we can do things that Jesus couldn't do, and we can go places He hadn't gone because we have more available to us. For example, through technology, the gospel message is brought to millions of people worldwide – through media sharing sites, television, and social media networks.

Moreover, the awesome ability of the greater works mantle anointing is reaching many through the empowerment of leadership. Under this kind of anointing, all excuses have been removed. God has given us boundless ability and opportunities to get His message out, and we must take advantage of them.

We have been infused with the power of Jesus Christ through the person of the Holy Spirit, and now we can go out and touch – change, influence, and affect – the world.

Feet Treading Mantle Anointing

A feet-treading mantle anointing is a possessive, territorial, and authoritative kind of anointing that claims rightful ownership to that which has already been predetermined by God. It is an anointing that enables an individual to step out and possess what God has promised. The way to activate this kind of anointing is by actually 'walking in it.'

In other words, the use of our feet coupled with bold unwavering faith in God's promises is necessary for this kind of mantle anointing. For example, in Joshua 1:3, God promised Joshua this 'possessive' kind of mantle anointing just as He said unto Moses. *"Every place that the sole of your foot shall tread [walk] upon, that I have given unto you..."* (Joshua 1:3, KJV; brackets added). We see a more descriptive verse in Deuteronomy 11:24, *"Wherever you set foot, that land will be yours. Your frontiers will stretch from the wilderness in the south to Lebanon in the north, and from the Euphrates River in the east to the Mediterranean Sea in the west"* (NLT). My point is, we won't possess what belongs to us until we have walked – placed our feet – on it in the spirit realm and naturally by the Lord's leading. Knowing this, we should to be more deliberate in claiming what's ours with our feet. Where we 'step' is what we get.

God was speaking directly to Joshua in Joshua 1:3. He told Joshua that the same kind of anointing that rested upon Moses to cause him to possess and claim the blessings of God would be evident in his life as well. Moses was dead, but the mantle anointing continued in the life of Joshua – a 'feet treading' mantle anointing! Additionally, God told Joshua that he would be a possessor through the activity and direction of his feet. Our feet are significant!

Although this was a promise to Joshua under the Old Covenant, we have the same anointed power today. According to Deuteronomy 11:24, this kind of anointing only comes upon those who are obedient to God. *"So that day Moses solemnly promised me, 'The land of Canaan on which you were just walking will be your grant of land and that of your descendants forever because you wholeheartedly followed the LORD my God.'"* (Joshua 14:9, NLT). The words *"...wholeheartedly followed the LORD my God..."* speaks of obedience. Obedience is a crucial factor in wearing the mantle anointing that causes one to possess.

Now, let us look at the feet treading mantle anointing promised to those under the new covenant. In Luke 10:19, Jesus said, *"Look, I have given you authority over all the power of the enemy, and you can walk among snakes and scorpions and crush them. Nothing will injure you"* (NLT).

The promise of Luke 10:19 is great, but it doesn't mean that we should literally seek out serpents and scorpions to walk on to test our authority or as some kind of ritual. There are religions that practice this act, but it is a foolish, demonic, and dangerous practice, and the Holy Bible does not support it! That verse simply means that through the power of the Holy Spirit, we can disarm and demolish the vices of the enemy in the spirit realm. We can pull down the strongholds of the enemy (II Corinthians 10:3-5). At times God will allow us to see in the natural realm what has been done as a result of our persistence – through the Holy Spirit's power – against the devil in the spirit realm.

Jesus Christ has given us authority over evil spirits so that when they try to overtake and defeat us, we can literally crush them under our feet by the power and authority of the Holy Spirit and through prayer. According to The Merriam-Webster Concise Dictionary, the word *"tread"* means to step or walk on or over.
To move on foot: dance; to beat or press with the feet; the manner or sound of stepping. Our feet have the ability to step, walk, dance, beat, and press. We do these things in the natural realm with our feet, but God applies these actions in the spirit realm to produce accordingly.

In Joshua 3:15-17, as the feet of the priests touched the Jordan River, the water divided so that the people could walk through on dry ground. These were not just ordinary feet; they were the feet of those who were consecrated, set apart, and holy unto God.

We can't use our feet to take us places where God forbids us to go, and then expect Him to bless us through the action of our feet. We must have holy feet and use them for holy purposes just like the priesthood of the Old Testament.

God gave instructions to Joshua to march around the wall of Jericho six times – once per day for six days. On the seventh day, he was to march around the wall seven times. Joshua and the people obeyed God's instructions, and on the seventh day, the wall came tumbling down! The anointing came as a result of their obedience to the instructions God gave them. How did the anointing come? He came in their feet (Joshua 6:1-5, 11-20). Possessive anointing was in their feet, and they took the city of Jericho. Doing everything else that God instructed them to do, such as ordering the people by rank, sounding the trumpet on the seventh day, and shouting with a great shout, wasn't enough. They had to use their feet to march around the wall; otherwise, they wouldn't get the victory.

We have 'feet treading' mantle anointing. Our feet are anointed to crush and destroy the evil forces, influences, and activities of the devil by the power of the Holy Spirit who indwells us.

Chapter 19: Obtaining the Mantle Anointing of Jesus Christ

Before looking at how to obtain the mantle anointing of Jesus Christ, it would be helpful to understand the unique anointing that worked in Jesus' life and in the lives of those He had chosen to equip and prepare with such an anointing. Let's begin by looking at Jesus' model.

The Model of Jesus: He Did It

The model of Jesus was a relational model. The most effective way to equip others to continue the work He had begun was by establishing relationships of empowerment. In doing so, Jesus was available and willing to serve those He had chosen to be in relationship with Him.

The disciples and apostles – whom I'll refer to interchangeably – must have felt very special to be chosen and to go through intensive training with the Savior. On the contrary, their relationship with Jesus also had its challenges. Just reading the gospel accounts of Jesus' relationship with His disciples show us that they suffered and were persecuted because of their stand for Christ and His gospel message. With their choice to follow Jesus came tremendous responsibility and consequences. I bet the disciples didn't realize – at first – that the demands were so great and that they would face trials, challenges, and difficulties in carrying out the work of the Kingdom.

Jesus didn't expect His disciples to operate under the same mantle anointing as He had without first equipping them and ensuring that they knew how to utilize the anointing. He did so by allowing them to observe His demonstration of the anointing as manifested in the lives of those He ministered to. Jesus modeled what He expected His disciples to do.

By such a demonstration, His disciples were able to have a clear understanding of the work and purpose of the anointing, including how to attract Him, keep Him, and utilize Him. There are those who learn through observation better than reading an instructional booklet on how to perform a particular task.

Expressions like 'talk is cheap,' 'walk the talk,' and 'practice what you preach' all mean the same thing, which leads to yet another expression – 'actions speak louder than words'! Of the latter two, Jesus did just that. He not only knew what to say, He knew what to do. His works backed up His words. He did it! In the same manner, we must conduct our lives so that others can read us – as living epistles – and not hear empty words that never amount to anything (II Corinthians 3:2-6). Just do it!

The Model of Jesus: Learning by Observation

Jesus knew the importance of having His disciples with Him as He went out to do the work of the Father. The only way they could learn was by being around the Thrower. Additionally, they needed to be with Him to see how He conducted Himself and for the purpose of building and strengthening their relationship with Him. They needed to understand Jesus' thought process and to be clear about His mission and purpose on earth. Such clarity and knowledge would provide a strong foundation upon which the disciples wouldn't be easily shaken, especially once they stepped out independent of having Jesus physically present with them.

Anyone who believes in something ought to know and be able to articulate precisely what that belief is, why that belief is held to, how that belief can be communicated to others, and the end results that having that belief will produce. *"Instead, you must worship Christ as Lord of your life. And if someone asks about your hope as a believer, always be ready to explain it. But do this in a gentle and respectful way"* (I Peter 3:5, NIV).

It's inadvisable to do anything of great importance without first counting the cost. Even Jesus supported this notion in His parable on self-denial found in the gospel of Luke 14:27-30, which reads, *"And if you do not carry your own cross and follow me, you cannot be my disciple. But don't begin until you count the cost. For who would begin construction of a building without first calculating the cost to see if there is enough money to finish it? Otherwise, you might complete only the foundation before running out of money, and then everyone would laugh at you. They would say, 'There's the person who started that building and couldn't afford to finish it!'"* (NLT – See also verses 31-33).

The Model of Jesus: He Let the Disciples Do It

The act of training involves showing an individual how to do a particular task and then allowing him or her to do it. This was Jesus' method of training the disciples. He showed them how, and then, eventually, He allowed them to go out on their own and do what they had observed Him do (Matthew 10; Matthew 11:1). In Matthew 10, Jesus gave His disciples a long lecture beginning with empowerment (verses 1-3, 8). He then set restrictions as to where they could and couldn't go (verses 5-6). He communicated clearly what their message should be, *"...preach, saying, 'The Kingdom of Heaven is at hand'"* (verse 7). He told them how to prepare themselves in terms of what they would and wouldn't need as they went out (verses 9-10). In Matthew 10:10, Jesus told His disciples not to prepare a written script of what they would say. This meant that the disciples had to know the work of the Lord and His message, having the same passion and burden for souls that Jesus had, and knowing how to articulate the reason for their hope.

In Matthew 10:11-14, Jesus cautioned His disciples about where they should lodge. He left no stone unturned.

He warned them about the kind of people they would encounter along the way – wolves (verse 16). Moreover, He told them that their mission would not be easy and that they would face opposition, rejection, and even physical persecution (verses 17-23). Jesus made sure that His disciples understood the full scope of what they were up against. As the last part of Jesus' lecture to His disciples, He comforted and assured them, telling them not to be afraid (verses 26-31).

Jesus wanted a wholehearted commitment from those who were empowered with His mantle (verses 37-39). He wanted His disciples to love Him more than they loved anyone else (verse 37) and certainly more than they loved the world and the things of the world. (See I John 2:15-17).

The Model of Jesus: Evangelize the World

Jesus came to win or save the lost – soul winning. He ensured that His disciples knew that was also their purpose. He was anointed to evangelize, and His disciples operated under the same anointing. They were able to pick up where He left off because they were divinely appointed and empowered to operate under this distinct type of anointing – and so are we!

Soul winning is winning souls to Christ, not to a particular church or denomination. As a result of soul winning, the local church experiences growth. When we invite people to church, soul-winning can occur as their hearts are pricked by the preached gospel of Jesus Christ or the authentic worship of God that takes place. However, inviting people to church shouldn't stop there. There must be follow-up with those individuals by the church as well as those who invited them.

Evangelism is the responsibility of every believer (Matthew 28:19-20; Acts 1:8; 8:1-4).

However, to win souls, we must have a burden and compassion for souls. Such a burden is what causes us to reach out to lost souls, bringing them into God's Kingdom. Proverbs 11:30 reads, *"The fruit of the righteous is a tree of life, and he who wins souls is wise"* (NKJV). There is a technique to soul-winning: prepare the soil before sowing the seed. For this reason, we must consider the amount of time we spend preparing people's hearts to receive Jesus Christ and the Word of God. Many people come into the church for the first time, whether on their own or by invitation. They hear the gospel message for the first time, and no sooner than the message is preached and the call to discipleship is made, they're expected to make an impromptu decision on whether or not they want to be saved. Granted, it can certainly happen this way but only if the Holy Spirit pricks the heart of the individual. Jesus said, *"No one comes to the Father except through Me"* (John 14:6, NKJV).

Adequate teaching and training are necessary as we draw others to Christ – that's relational and why follow-up is so important. If individuals aren't taught why they need to accept Christ as their Savior and how to grow in relationship with Him once they've accepted Him, then they will soon fade (Matthew 13).

Evangelizing requires the power of our personal testimony; this is very important (I Peter 3:15). We must be ready and willing to share with others what the Lord has done for us.
Our personal testimony is one of the most effective ways in which we can lead others to Christ. People need to know that we were wretched, blinded by the darkness of the god of this world, lost in sin, servants to the lust of our flesh, and destined to a burning hell – until Jesus reached down into the muck and mire of sin and lifted us out by His love and mercy. We are saved by grace (Ephesians 2:8-9). They don't only need to hear us quoting scripture verses. Where is our transparency?

In sharing our personal testimonies, we should take into consideration the effect our testimonies *may* have on others, how much of our testimonies to share, the right time to share, and for what purpose – none other than them experiencing the unconditional love of God.

Before we can effectively evangelize, we must get people's attention. Before Jesus started witnessing to the woman at the well in John 4:7-42, He got her attention by talking about something she was interested in. He identified the common ground. I talk about this in detail in my daily devotional book entitled, *Reset with God*, so I won't do so here. Bombarding or attacking others by talking about theology and points of salvation will do nothing more than turn them off or incite anger. When people's hearts and minds become closed because of our ignorance and lack of compassion in how we approach them, they won't receive what we have to say. On the contrary, once we get an individual's interest, then that person will begin asking questions.

Many people already have a desire to live for God, so we don't have to create the desire in them – we can't. We only need to help them recognize the desire that's already there, build upon it, and let *that* desire be the vehicle that the Lord uses to draw them.

It's easy – and detrimental – to condemn people while witnessing to them, making them feel guilty and convicted of their sins and unworthy of God's love and forgiveness. Let's remember that we were once condemned but through God's grace and mercy, He removed from us the feeling of guilt and shame when we accepted Christ as Lord and Savior. As we walk in the Spirit, there's no more condemnation (Romans 8:1).

Condemning others when witnessing to them – intentionally or unintentionally – causes their hearts to close to the message of Christ.

Another aspect of witnessing that makes it is easy to fall into error is competing with and criticizing other churches, pastors, and denominations in the presence of the prospect rather than just sticking to the gospel message, which is what will draw that person to Christ.

Evangelism is so critical that it's worth revisiting the scriptures to see how it should be done so we can more effectively win others to Christ. See the following scriptures on soul-winning: Acts 8:26-40 – the Ethiopian Eunuch; Luke 5:17-26 – the man with palsy; Luke 19:2-10 – conversion of Zacharias; John 3:1-21 – Nicodemus; John 4:1-26, 39-42 – the woman at the well; Acts 16:23-34 – the Philippian jailer; Acts 26:1-32 – Paul witnessed to King Agrippa. The main purpose for which we have been robed with the mantle anointing of Jesus Christ is to evangelize the world!

The one who has not yet obtained the mantle anointing of Jesus Christ can do so by accepting Him as Savior, earnestly following Him, holding to His teachings in obedience, and accepting Bible truth by faith.

Belief in and of itself is not enough unless it moves one to action. It's challenging to develop a relationship with someone without having faith in him or her. On the contrary, once the belief factor is present, an individual can proceed further, taking the necessary steps to know more about the one he or she believes in. Some will do whatever it takes to acquaint themselves with others in hopes of adapting their admirable traits.

They will pursue them – throwers – until throwers become an active part of their lives. At best, pursuers – catchers – will try to connect with what throwers are connected to.

Once the belief factor is present in others, we can start building upon it. Some of the obvious ways to know Jesus Christ is through the Bible, prayer, and by fellowshipping with others who have come to know Him. One of the most powerful ways to get to know Christ is to call on Him through prayer. Calling upon the Lord is a way of asking Him to come into or be a part of our lives, and there is a promise given in scripture that whoever calls on the name of the Lord will be saved – delivered, set free from whatever holds them captive (Romans 10:13). Romans 10:14 reads, *"How then shall they call on him in whom they have not believed? And how shall they believe in him of whom they have not heard? And how shall they hear without a preacher"* (KJV). Those who have not accepted Christ can receive His mantle anointing by allowing Him to come into their hearts. This anointing is available to everyone, but the sad truth is not everyone will receive Him. Friend, I pray that you have made a choice to receive Jesus Christ as your Lord and Savior and that you join a Bible-believing church and get grounded in the Bible and serve the Lord.

Receiving Christ isn't complicated; one only needs to follow the prescription that the Bible gives – confess with your mouth that Jesus is Lord and believe with your heart that He will come into your life, and He will do just that (Romans 10:8-10, 13). Furthermore, confession is an important aspect of salvation, which means acknowledging one's sinful nature, which we all were born with (Psalm 51:5), making a conscious decision to turn from that destructive nature, and receiving one's God-nature, which Christ died that we might have.

Our God-nature emerges once we invite Jesus Christ into our hearts, completely submitting to Him. Although He no longer exists in human form, He exists in the person of the Holy Spirit (John 14:15-18). A life that is led by the Holy Spirit is far better than a life controlled by the god of this world (Romans 8:1-13; John 4:24; II Corinthians 4:4). Satan robbed us of our ability to live according to our God-nature, but through the redemptive work of Jesus Christ, He stood up to Satan, looked him square in the eyes, snatched everything that was stolen from us out of Satan's hands so that we could be free to serve God.

Those desiring to turn to Jesus Christ can do so by turning their back on sin; thereby, gaining power and authority over sin through Christ (Colossians 2:13-15). If you're without the Lord as Savior, He's ready to throw His mantle anointing on you. Receive Him today. If you've already accepted the Lord Jesus Christ, but you haven't committed to walking with Him daily and serving Him, I plead with you to do so and receive His mantle anointing. His anointing will empower you with His characteristics – as you adapt His ways – so that you can fulfill His purpose for your life.

The Lord's mantle anointing won't wear out, weaken, or fade. He cannot be defeated, overthrown, or dethroned as the King of kings and Lord of lords. We, on the other hand, have the responsibility of protecting and nurturing the anointing through prayer, Bible reading, holy living – including worship, praise, thanksgiving, and gathering with Christian believers in fellowship.

Let me be clear, the anointing doesn't need protection because He is weak or vulnerable; instead, we need to protect His anointing in us as fragile clay jars, prone to wander and leave the One we love (II Corinthians 4:7-9).

The anointing of Jesus Christ – the Holy Spirit – is a Treasure given to us. If we take care of this mantle anointing, guarding it against foreign objects, infiltration, and invasion of darkness, then He will grow more powerful, become more beautiful, illustrious, and illuminated in us day by day.

There's nothing better than being filled with the Holy Spirit and living a victorious life free from sin. The Bible teaches that we have a choice whether to be free or remain in bondage. If we yield – submit or subject – our mind and body as servants to sin, then we are held captive by sin. But if we yield our members as servants to righteousness, then we are free from the bondage of sin. There's no guarantee that doing so will automatically cause sin to be removed from our lives (Romans 3:23). Becoming a Christian believer doesn't make us exempt from sinning. The flesh wars against the spirit (Ephesians 6; II Corinthians 10:3-5; Romans 8:12-14). The good news is that sin can't have power over us – unless we yield to it. Jesus provided the antidote for victory over temptation: maintaining a watchful spirit and praying (Matthew 26:41).

Becoming a Christian believer enables us to gain power or control over sin through Jesus Christ our Lord. If it was possible to have power over sin without the help of Jesus Christ, we wouldn't need Him, but He takes what's impossible for us to do in our own strength and makes it possible when He enters our lives (Zechariah 4:6).

There is a mantle anointing hanging in Heaven's closet with your name on it. The designer is God Himself. Will you call upon the Lord and ask Him for your mantle anointing? As I stated earlier, the Bible teaches that whoever calls on the name of the Lord will, undoubtedly, be saved. Salvation is that simple! If you're tired of living in sin, confess those sins before the Lord.

Make Him your High Priest (Hebrews 4:15-16) by completely turning away from your sins. An invitation is extended to you today. If you're tired of sin and its adverse effects in your life and the lives of those you love, then you're a perfect candidate for salvation.

Being saved – believing in the resurrected Christ and confessing the same – and leading a disciplined life of obedience and total surrender to Christ and the Bible ensures us a place in Heaven's mansions. That doesn't mean we won't ever sin, but it does mean we are empowered to live free from sin. *If* we do sin, we have an advocate with the Father – Jesus Christ. We must quickly and sincerely repent, turning away from the practice of sinning.

Some people think once they make the initial step to becoming a Christian believer, they don't have to do anything more to grow in and maintain this lifestyle. They think everything will be perfect and fall into place, but that couldn't be further from the truth. This belief system is both false and dangerous. Even after becoming a Christian, we must work on our salvation daily – work *on* it, not *for* it (Ephesians 2:8-9; Philippians 2:12-13). One who's in possession of something valuable and irreplaceable takes the time to guard it, keeping it safe and secure, and doing whatever is necessary to preserve it. We must take the same stand with regards to salvation. Salvation with all of its benefits is a priceless, invaluable treasure which we 'house' in our bodies, and we can't afford to take our eyes off this treasure (II Corinthians 4:6-7; Psalm 103:1-5; Psalm 116:12-14, 17).

Jesus made a comforting promise to everyone that would believe in Him: where He lives, they will one day live. That place is the Father's House – Heaven (John 14:1-3). We're just pilgrims passing through this life for a brief moment. Our most earnest possession is in heaven.

The Bible teaches that where a person's treasure is, that's where his or her heart is (Matthew 6:19-21). Our treasure shouldn't be comprised of earthly substance and material wealth but, instead, heavenly substance and spiritual wealth. It's up to us to ensure that we don't lose the treasure God has given us, which is our most earnest possession. In the Gospel of Matthew, we're admonished to make sure there's oil in our lamp and that the oil doesn't run out.

This admonishment comes because when the Bridegroom – Jesus Christ – returns for His bride – the church – the oil – Holy Spirit – in our lamp will be the identifying factor, quickening us to be 'caught up' with the Bridegroom (Matthew 25:1-13). The Holy Spirit will be our access into heaven. We can look forward to a honeymoon like no other! In this life, some may never experience a wedding, honeymoon, or married life, but every Christian believer who remains in a state of readiness will experience a honeymoon that is literally 'out of this world'!

That glorious day is coming, but we must prepare for it now. We don't know exactly when the honeymoon will take place, which is all the more reason to be ready at all times (Matthew 24:32-44). We can't allow the Bridegroom to come for us and find us still in bed – in a state of spiritual sleep and slumber, still dabbling in sin – without oil in our lamps. As the bride of Christ, we must arise, get in and remain in our rightful place by putting on the mantle anointing of Jesus Christ! (See James 4:7-10; Ephesians 5:10-20).

Again, I plead with you, if you don't know the Lord in the pardon of your sins, make a conscious decision today to accept Him. Give Him your heart, your life. Today is the day of salvation. Repeat this prayer sincerely and turn from your sins to follow Christ.

Lord Jesus, I know I was conceived with a sin-nature, but I no longer want this nature, especially since I now know that you died so that I might have the nature of my Father in Heaven. I'm tired of yielding to what this world wants and to my selfish and destructive desires. I no longer want the nature of the "god of this world,' Satan. Come, Lord Jesus and live in my heart, for I have reserved a place for You. I am ready for my life to be changed according to God's plan and purpose for me. I no longer make apologies for my sins; I am now in a place of true repentance and am ready to make a complete turnaround. I confess with my mouth that Jesus Christ is Lord and believe in my heart that God raised Him from the dead. Thank you, Lord, for saving me. Come now and fill me with Your Holy Spirit and transform my life through the power of your Word. Give me a never-ending desire for communion with You and Your Word and cause me to grow in relationship with You as I begin my pursuit to follow You. Thank you, Lord, for hearing my prayer today and for working in me so I may arise to take my rightful place as Your bride, to walk in the newness of life that You bring. In Jesus' name. Amen.

Friend, from this day forward, build a relationship with Christ and walk with Him daily, growing in grace and the knowledge of Christ. It's worth it! Find a Bible-believing, teaching, preaching, praying, and worshipping church and attend services regularly. Get around strong believers who are grounded in the Bible and in faith and serve in the local church.

We have been called into a mantle anointing relationship with Jesus Christ, and we ought to do everything necessary to ensure that His mantle continues to rest upon us and resides in us – that we don't grieve the Holy Spirit by our lifestyle and disobedience (Ephesians 4:30). We have received an invaluable, tangible, endowment, and endorsement, enabling us to move forward in doing God's work that He may be glorified by all of those who look on (Matthew 5:16).

Let's rise up *in* Christ because there's no greater mantle anointing than what we have been given. We are anointed, appointed, and empowered 'for such a time as this' (Esther 4:14). *"Now unto him that is able to keep you from falling, and to present you faultless before the presence of his glory with exceeding joy, to the only wise God our Savior, be glory and majesty, dominion and power, both now and ever. Amen"* (Jude v.v. 24-25, KJV).

Thank You

To my readers, thank you so much for supporting this work. **I trust that this book has been a blessing to you and ask that you kindly leave a professional, positive review on Amazon.com.**

To be kept informed of my latest and upcoming works, please visit my website at www.drjudysbookstudio.com and sign up for email notifications. There you may also send me a message, or you may email me directly at dr.judybookstudio@gmail.com.

Other Literary Works by The Author

♦ The Virtuous Woman: Her Price Is Far Above Rubies (2000)
Sold out

♦ Mantle Anointing (First printing – 2002)
Sold out

♦ Worship Leading (2004) ~ Textbook
Sold out

♦ Worship: Becoming What We See (2010)
Available on Amazon.com

♦ Reset with God (2020) ~ 30-Day Daily Devotional with a 16-page Bonus Section
Available on Amazon.com

Website: www.drjudysbookstudio.com
Email: dr.judybookstudio@gmail.com
Follow Dr. Judy on Social Media

Made in the USA
Middletown, DE
09 May 2023